GALAXY 4

DOCTOR WHO *THE SCRIPTS*: GALAXY 4
ISBN 1 85286 566 0

Published by
Titan Books Ltd
42-44 Dolben Street
London SE1 0UP

First edition July 1994
10 9 8 7 6 5 4 3 2 1

British Library Cataloguing-in-Publication Data. A catalogue record for
this book is available from the British Library.

By arrangement with BBC Books, a division of BBC Enterprises Ltd.

Printed and bound in Great Britain by Cox and Wyman Ltd, Reading,
Berkshire.

For Mum and Dad

GALAXY 4
WILLIAM EMMS

EDITED BY JOHN McELROY

TITAN BOOKS
LONDON

CONTENTS

INTRODUCTION

Most people reading this book will undoubtedly be aware that a large number of classic early *Doctor Who* episodes are 'missing' - in other words, the BBC no longer holds copies of these episodes in a viewable or transmittable form. One of the earliest Script Books, *Tomb of the Cybermen,* was such a lost classic when the book was first published, but then all four episodes were dramatically recovered and quickly released by BBC Enterprises on video for all to enjoy.

What is perhaps less known is that, despite the large number of missing episodes, audio recordings of most of these *do* still exist, thanks to the diligence and dedication of a few fans of the programme who, week after week, recorded each episode on their reel-to-reel machines while the rest of us merely watched.

It is thanks to these people, and Richard Landen in particular, that BBC Enterprises have been able to release audio recordings of a number of legendary *Doctor Who* stories - *Power of the Daleks*, *Evil of the Daleks*, *The Macra Terror, Fury from the Deep* - hopefully with more to come.

Over the years some fans have managed to acquire unofficial copies of most of these missing stories. However, there are two notable exceptions, *The Crusade* by David Whitaker and *Galaxy 4* by William Emms, and we decided therefore that both of these deserved to be published in Script Book form as soon as possible. As you will probably know, one episode of *The Crusade* (episode three - *The Wheel of Fortune*) does exist on video, and has been commercially released as part of *The Hartnell Years* videotape. We have therefore given priority to *Galaxy 4*.

It is interesting to note that, back in the mid 1970s, the Doctor Who Appreciation Society was in negotiation with the BBC to show a complete story at one of their first conventions, and *Galaxy 4* was chosen. The BBC insisted that the permission of every person connected with the programme be sought before it could be shown. Despite the best efforts of the society's executive committee, they failed to get all the required permissions in time and, as a result, *Galaxy 4* was not shown. A few short months after this, the programme was destroyed - perhaps lost forever.

With previous Script Books, we have used the actual recorded version as the basis for each book. Obviously with *Galaxy 4* this was not possible, and the script section of the book is taken directly from the copy of the script that the BBC holds. During the course of preparing this book for publication, a fairly bad audio copy of episode two, *Trap of Steel,* was located, and this has been compared to the script version. There *are* differences between the two, but I think it is fair to say that they are very minor. The basic flow of the script is identical, each scene and each actor's lines are in the same place, although it can be seen that a lot of the first Doctor's way of speaking came from William Hartnell rather than from the script writers. For example, the "my dear child"s so common when the first Doctor spoke to his companions, are present in the audio version, whilst notably absent in the script version.

Another difference worth noting is that in the opening scene the script describes the surface of the planet as follows: 'trees and plant life spring in abundant quantity'. In the television version, a little sparse vegetation was all that could be seen. Whether this was due to budget limitations or, perhaps more likely, because it was felt that a dying planet should not have an abundance of lush vegetation, is unknown. Also, the Chumblies are said to make various *chittering* and *chumbling* sounds in the script, but as far as we can tell, in the televised version they made no sound at all.

There are people who will doubtless demand to know why both versions were not included in the book, and this was indeed considered. In the end, though, we could not justify including two such similar versions, particularly when portions of the audio version were completely unintelligible.

All we can hope is that some day this story, like *Tomb of the Cybermen*, will be recovered and we will all be able to watch it for ourselves. Perhaps, even as you read this, a copy is sitting on some dusty shelf in the vaults of a far-off TV station...

John McElroy, May 1994

BACKGROUND

Galaxy 4 was the opening story of *Doctor Who*'s third season. Its first episode went out in the series' regular Saturday teatime slot on 11th September 1965, just seven weeks after the previous season finished its run with the final episode of *The Time Meddler*. It had in fact been made directly after *The Time Meddler* as the final story of the second production block, but was held in reserve to launch the new season.

Behind the scenes, this was a period of transition for *Doctor Who*. The original producer, Verity Lambert, was now nearing the end of her involvement with the series and, although she still received the on-screen credit, her successor John Wiles had by this time taken over much of the responsibility. Similarly, although season two's story editor Dennis Spooner commissioned *Galaxy 4*, his replacement Donald Tosh was firmly in charge by the time it went into production, only in this case it was the newcomer who received the on-screen credit.

John Wiles had moved to England in 1949 from his native South Africa. He joined the BBC in the early fifties as a staffwriter/adapter in the Script Department after his play, *The Dancing Bear* (co-written with Richard Wade), was accepted for production. Later he became a story editor, working first on series such as the soap opera *Compact* and then, in 1964, on thriller serials for the recently launched BBC2. At the same time, he developed a parallel career as a director in the theatre. He was promoted to producer by BBC Head of Serials Donald Wilson, and shortly afterwards was asked to take over *Doctor Who* from Verity Lambert, whose office was just down the corridor from his in Union House, a BBC-owned building overlooking Shepherd's Bush Green in

London. Lambert, after three years in the post, was now keen to seek fresh challenges. She went on to launch two new series, *The Newcomers* and *Adam Adamant Lives!*, before leaving the BBC in the late sixties to continue her career with the rival ITV network. Today her Cinema Verity organisation is one of the UK's leading independent production houses.

Donald Tosh began his career in the theatre, but in the mid-fifties joined Granada TV where, amongst many other projects, he discovered the format for the series which became *Coronation Street*. After six years he moved to the BBC and, despite earlier suggestions that he would be assigned to the classic serials, found himself working as story editor on *Compact*. After eighteen months of this he was offered the chance to transfer either to another bi-weekly serial or to *Doctor Who*. He chose *Doctor Who*.

The writer of *Galaxy 4* was William Emms, another newcomer to the series, who was commissioned on the basis of an unsolicited story outline he had sent on to the production office. He had turned to writing four years earlier after beginning his career as an English teacher in London's East End, and had already been responsible for numerous one-off plays as well as several adaptions and occasional series episodes. Brought up on the stories of H.G. Wells, he was a great admirer of science fiction and had watched *Doctor Who* regularly before contributing to it.

The story that Emms came up with, under the initial working title of *The Chumblies*, was an entertaining if relatively straightforward morality tale. It saw the Doctor and his companions arriving on an arid planet in *Galaxy*

4 and meeting the respective occupants of two crashed spaceships; a group of handsome male humanoids called Drahvins and a party of hideous reptilian creatures known as Rills. Confounding audience expectations, the Rills would prove to be friendly, intelligent explorers whose robot servants, nicknamed Chumblies, serve only a peaceful purpose, while the Drahvins turn out to be a troop of mindless cloned soldiers terrorised by a warlike leader named Gar.

The director originally assigned to the story was Mervyn Pinfield, a veteran technical expert whose BBC career stretched back to the earliest days of the television service and who acted as associate producer on *Doctor Who* during its first year of production. One important change made at the casting stage was the transformation of the Drahvins from handsome men into beautiful women. This gave the story added impact at a time when the feminist movement, then more popularly known as 'women's lib', was much in the news, and also focused even greater emphasis upon the deceptive physical contrast between the attractiveness of the Drahvins and the ugliness of the Rills. A few minor changes were made to the scripts to reflect the change, including the addition of some darkly humorous dialogue in the first episode to indicate the Drahvins' contemptuous attitude towards men. Also the Drahvin leader's name was changed from Gar to Maaga.

Shooting got underway at the BBC's Television Film Studios in Ealing. The story's pre-filming allocation being used to achieve some scenes set on the planet's landscape for episode one, and a fight sequence between the Drahvins and the Chumblies for episode four, as well as a few assorted visual effects shots. As filming got underway it became clear that failing health would prevent Pinfield from completing his work on the story. A replacement was consequently enlisted in the person of Derek Martinus, who had only just completed the internal BBC directors' course and who had no previous practical experience of handling a TV production.

Born in 1931, Martinus had started his career in the theatre. He had worked for three years in Croydon, directing and acting in the round, and then had spells in Sheffield, Lincoln and Birmingham. After spending some time in Salisbury, Rhodesia (now Zimbabwe) he returned to England and, in 1965, joined the BBC.

"I came off the BBC course," he now recalls, "and there was a panic on. The *Doctor Who* director, Mervyn Pinfield, had fallen ill or something, and filming of his story had already started at Ealing Studios. It was suggested that I might take over.

"I'd not seen many episodes of the series at that time, so I was given an intensive course on what *Doctor Who* was all about. I sat down and watched some episodes, and Verity Lambert, the producer, asked me what I thought. I shocked her by commenting that I thought we should aim for higher standards! It was obviously not the thing to say, but when you're young and eager, and just off the course, you have high ideals." Despite this *faux pas*, Lambert confirmed that she would like Martinus to take over the reins on *Galaxy 4*.

"It was a strange situation," says Martinus, "because Mervyn was supposed to be sick but he was still there working on the production, and I was alongside him making suggestions. The show had all been cast, and the costumes were all made, and they had been shooting at Ealing for several days. I prepared my own camera scripts for the studio work and it was a very quick indoctrination into television."

Two of the most memorable aspects of the production were the Rills and their Chumbley robots. The Rills, vaguely resembling wart-hogs, were seen lurking in their spaceship behind glass screens and swathed in ammonia gas: in reality dry ice (carbon dioxide). Four costumes were made out of fibreglass and rubber. They were grey-green in colour and each large enough to house an actor who could operate the creature's arm-like appendages and thereby bring some movement to its otherwise static form. One late change was that actor Anthony Paul, who was originally to provide the Rills' voices, was unable to do so and was replaced by Robert Cartland. Paul, however, was still credited for episode three in the BBC listings magazine *Radio Times*, as it was by then too late for the entry to be amended.

The Chumblies' distinctive domed shape was devised by scenic designer Richard Hunt, partly with a view to possible merchandising potential. Again, four were made. Each was around three foot tall and had a basic structure consisting of a fibreglass shell mounted on castors to allow easy movement across the studio floor. A small light was positioned at the top to indicate when the Chumbley was in communication with its Rill masters, and several rod-like arm attachments were fixed between the dome sections to represent ray-guns, mechanical grips and other instruments as specified in the scripts. A number of pendulum-like objects, rather like bell clappers, were suspended around the base of the robot to represent its motor-units. Whenever a Chumbley was attacked or deactivated, its dome sections collapsed on top of each other; these shots were achieved by way of a dummy version constructed especially for the purpose.

"I remember that the Chumblies were played by midget actors, little tiny guys," says Derek Martinus. "They had a hard time as it was damned hot inside those fibreglass shells, and they could only just get inside them."

Martinus remembers that he was keen to demonstrate his creative abilities on this, his début production.

"I recall that I had great ambitions for doing long tracking shots and developing shots and all that sort of thing. I was rehearsing a scene and had told the cameraman to lay some tracks down on the set floor, but then I saw him setting up on another set entirely. I asked him what he was doing and he commented that as I hadn't told him much about the shot, he just wanted to get started. So I asked him which shot he was setting up for, and he said it was a close-up of William Hartnell, because his training was always to point the camera where the money was! I asked if he would mind doing my tracking shot first!

"For the closing sequence of the destruction of the planet, I seem to remember that we played the film in reverse, It was a lot of fun to shoot. The planet first exploded and then imploded."

Many *Doctor Who* directors, particularly those lacking in television experience, found the series' lead actor, William Hartnell, difficult to work with. Martinus was well aware of his reputation.

"Hartnell was very quick to size me up; he did that

with all the new directors. He was a pretty formidable figure, with a good track record in films, and he liked to present himself as an imposing, knowledgable sort of guy. He definitely liked to be the star."

One factor which may have complicated matters on *Galaxy 4* was that none of the three regular cast members was particularly happy with William Emms' scripts. Emms later recalled that both Hartnell and Maureen O'Brien (Vicki) had argued with him about their respective parts; and Peter Purves (Steven) had said that, as the story was originally written with the previous companions Ian and Barbara in mind, he was inappropriately given a lot of Barbara's dialogue and action - including being overpowered by Maaga in a fight. This may also have been a hangover from the fact that the Drahvins were originally to have been male characters.

Predictably, a guest cast of beautiful young women helped to secure *Galaxy 4* some good publicity in the popular press, where reports highlighted their evil nature, thus giving away one of the main plot twists, and described their distinctive green-and-white costumes and their striking make-up, complete with rows of blue sequins for eyebrows. The story was very well received by the general public, too, averaging 9,900,000 viewers per episode, the highest ratings of the whole season, as well as achieving a respectable appreciation figure of fifty-five per cent.

Following completion of work on *Galaxy 4*, Derek Martinus and his team went straight on to make the following episode, *Mission to the Unknown*, which was treated to all intents and purposes as part of the same production. This episode was unique in the series' history in that it featured none of the principal cast. Instead, it took the form of a one-off prologue to the epic twelve-parter *The Daleks' Master Plan*, which would effectively dominate the early part of the third season. That, however, is a different story...

Stephen James Walker, April 1994
With acknowledgments to David Gibbes-Auger, David J. Howe, Derek Martinus and Mark Stammers.

CAST

The Doctor...................... William Hartnell

Vicki.............................. Maureen O'Brien

Steven Taylor.................. Peter Purves

Maaga............................ Stephanie Bidmead

Drahvin One.................... Marina Martin

Drahvin Two................... Susanna Carroll

Drahvin Three................. Lyn Ashley

Chumblies...................... Angelo Muscat

Jimmy Kaye (Episode 1)

William Shearer (Episodes 2-4)

Pepi Poupee (Episodes 3-4)

Tommy Reynolds (Episode 4)

Rill voice....................... Robert Cartland (Episodes 3-4)

Rills.............................. Bill Lodge (Episodes 3-4)

Brian Madge (Episode 4)

Peter Holmes (Episode 4)

Bill McAllister (Episode 4)

Garvey........................... Barry Jackson (Episode 4)

TECHNICAL DETAILS

Story code: T
Story title: Galaxy 4
Working title: The Chumblies
Author: William Emms
Number of episodes: 4
Studios: R4 (Episodes 1-3)
                  TC3 (Episode 4)
                  Ealing (film inserts)

Episode One
Title.................................. Four Hundred Dawns
Duration........................... 22'21"
Recorded.......................... 9th July 1965
Transmitted...................... 11th September 1965, at 17:41
Viewing figure................. 9,000,000
Audience appreciation
figure............................... 56

Episode Two
Title.................................. Trap of Steel
Duration........................... 24'51"
Recorded.......................... 16th July 1965
Transmitted...................... 18th September 1965, at 17:50
Viewing figure................. 9,500,000
Audience appreciation
figure............................... 55

Episode Three
Title.................................. Air Lock
Duration........................... 24'19"
Recorded........................... 23rd July 1965
Transmitted...................... 25th September 1965, at 17:52
Viewing figure................ 11,300,000
Audience appreciation
figure............................... 54

Episode Four
Title.................................. The Exploding Planet
Duration........................... 24'47"
Recorded........................... 30th July 1965
Transmitted...................... 2nd October 1965, at 17:50
Viewing figure................ 9,900,000
Audience appreciation
figure............................... 53

PRODUCTION CREDITS

Producers............................ Verity Lambert
                                    John Wiles (uncredited)
Directors............................ Derek Martinus
                                    Mervyn Pinfield (uncredited)
Script editors...................... Donald Tosh
                                    Dennis Spooner (uncredited)
Production assistant........... Angela Gordon
Assistant floor manager..... Marjorie Yorke
Secretary........................... Sue Willis
Floor assistant.................... Nick Wright
Wardrobe supervisor.......... Daphne Dare
Make-up supervisor............ Sonia Markham
Designer............................ Richard Hunt
Vision mixer....................... Clive Doig
Technical operations
managers............................ Ralph Walton
                                    Derek Holiday
                                    Bernard Fox
Sound supervisor................ George Prince
Special sound..................... Brian Hodgson
Grams operator................... Richard Worby
Camera crew....................... Number Fourteen Crew

EPISODE ONE

FOUR HUNDRED DAWNS

1. EXTERIOR (DAY).

(A landscape on a planet in Galaxy 4. The smooth ground seems to be covered with a black, asphalt tarmac; splits have occurred in this smooth surface, and from these, trees and plant life spring in abundant quantity. The level of the ground is broken by large rock formations, craggy, but apparently made of the same material as the ground. Vegetation also pushes its way out of gaps in these rocks. It presents a peaceful scene, and all is quiet, no sound of life at all. The silence is broken as the TARDIS materialises.)

2. INTERIOR THE TARDIS.

(STEVEN and VICKI watch THE DOCTOR as he switches off the TARDIS controls with his usual evident satisfaction. STEVEN is

seated and VICKI *is cutting his hair.)*

VICKI: Arrived, have we?

THE DOCTOR: We have, my dear.

STEVEN: Good, where?

THE DOCTOR: We'll be able to see that when I get the scanner on, won't we?

                  (As he speaks, THE DOCTOR *moves to switch on the scanner.)*

                  There we are. Now you can take a look.

                  *(*THE DOCTOR *points up at the scanner.* VICKI *looks as he indicates. They study the picture.)*

STEVEN: Where are we, Doctor? Is it a planet you recognise?

                  *(*STEVEN *starts to get up.)*

VICKI: Keep still...

THE DOCTOR: Be quiet. Listen, both of you.

                  *(*THE DOCTOR *waves them to be quiet and adjusts some controls.* STEVEN *and* VICKI *listen.)*

STEVEN: Listen to what? I can't hear anything.

THE DOCTOR: Exactly. Exactly. There's not a sound out there, no sound at all.

                  *(*THE DOCTOR *turns to look up at the*

scanner. The others follow his gaze.)

Just silence.

3. *EXTERIOR.*

(The silence is overpowering, strange. No bird song, no stirring in the trees.)

4. *INTERIOR THE TARDIS.*

(VICKI and STEVEN turn from the scanner and give their attention to THE DOCTOR, who is fussing with the dials and switches of the control console.)

THE DOCTOR: Atmospheric pressure, temperature, oxygen content, radiation... all normal. I wonder...

(THE DOCTOR looks up at the scanner.)

... if it's possible to have a planet so obviously conducive to life, yet... without any.

VICKI: Well, I've finished chopping this fellow. Can we go out and see?

THE DOCTOR: I don't see why not. It appears completely deserted. It seems as though we've at last got a chance of some undisturbed peace.

5. *EXTERIOR.*

(From behind a cluster of black rocks, near the TARDIS, comes a chattering and jingling sound. Suddenly a CHUMBLEY *appears on the rocky slope above and stops. The* CHUMBLEY *fidgets this way and that, then faces the police box. For a moment it chatters to itself.)*

6. *INTERIOR THE TARDIS.*

STEVEN: That's marvellous. I hope there's a lake or river nearby. Fancy a swim, Doctor?

THE DOCTOR: What do you think this is - a joy ride? This is a scientific expedition.

STEVEN: Oh, come on Doctor. You can't be scientific all the time. You look as if you could do with a wash!

VICKI: The Doctor in cold water!

THE DOCTOR: From past experience, young man, you have always to be on your guard.

STEVEN: Well, I'm willing to take the risk.

7. *EXTERIOR.*

(The CHUMBLEY *moves towards the TARDIS and bumps into it.)*

8. *INTERIOR THE* TARDIS.

(THE DOCTOR, STEVEN *and* VICKI *all jump at the sound of the collision.*)

VICKI: What was that?

STEVEN: Well, I'm ready...

            (*He is interrupted by a further bump.*)

THE DOCTOR: Shh!

9. *EXTERIOR*.

(*The* CHUMBLEY *bumps into the* TARDIS *yet again, chitters and jingles, then slowly turns to the right, all the time keeping in contact with the outside of the ship. When it is in line with the side, it moves forward, constantly bumping the side, obviously feeling its way along. At the corner it stops, makes various little noises, then nudges its way around and proceeds along that side.*)

10. *INTERIOR THE* TARDIS.

(THE DOCTOR, VICKI *and* STEVEN *are standing and listening. The sounds can clearly be heard within the ship.*)

STEVEN: What's going on?

VICKI: There's something feeling its way around

the ship.

THE DOCTOR: Yes... like something discovering by touch. Something blind.

(VICKI *moves around, facing the sound of the noise.*)

VICKI: It's reaching the corner.

(*The bumping and sliding noise stops. For a moment there is silence, followed by a series of taps as the* CHUMBLEY *re-orientates itself. Then the bumping and sliding sounds starts again.*)

THE DOCTOR: Yes, it's blind.

VICKI: Whatever it is.

THE DOCTOR: As you say, whatever it is.

11. EXTERIOR.

(*The* CHUMBLEY *bumbles its way around the last corner of the TARDIS. It stops, chitters to itself, then moves off to a distance of about six feet.*)

12. INTERIOR THE TARDIS.

(*As the* CHUMBLEY *moves away, it comes into view on the scanner screen. The* CHUMBLEY *stops, a light starts flashing on top of it and it starts to emit a high-*

pitched, whistling sound.)

THE DOCTOR: Fascinating. Now that's something different.

*(*THE DOCTOR *and his two companions continue to stare at the scanner.)*

STEVEN: It looks to me as though it's sending a message.

THE DOCTOR: Yes. To its controllers. Whoever they are...

STEVEN: Or, whatever they are...

*(*VICKI *shakes* THE DOCTOR's *arm, and points back to the screen. The* CHUMBLEY *is slowly moving away.)*

VICKI: Look how it moves. It's got a sort of 'chumbley' movement.

STEVEN: Chumbley?

VICKI: Yes, can't you see? All sort of... chumbley.

(They turn away from the scanner. The CHUMBLEY *is now out of sight.)*

THE DOCTOR: Well, he's gone now.

STEVEN: Bang goes our swimming.

VICKI: Doesn't take much to put you off.

THE DOCTOR: Mmm, so I was wrong. Not only is there life here, but it's intelligent, highly intelligent to build a machine like that.

VICKI: A Chumbley.

THE DOCTOR: Very well, child... a Chumbley.

                  (THE DOCTOR turns to the control panel and flicks some switches and levers.)

STEVEN: Those things might be dangerous.

THE DOCTOR: I intend to find out about them. Open the doors...

                  (THE DOCTOR operates a control and the TARDIS doors swing open. THE DOCTOR picks up his stick and starts to leave. STEVEN and VICKI exchange a slightly worried glance, but still follow him.)

                  13. EXTERIOR.

                  (THE DOCTOR comes out of the TARDIS, followed by STEVEN and then VICKI. THE DOCTOR stands and sniffs the air.)

THE DOCTOR: Delightful. Just the right oxygen content.

VICKI: I can smell flowers.

THE DOCTOR: Indeed, indeed, delightful. And there are no... 'Chumblies' about.

                  (THE DOCTOR moves back and locks the door of the TARDIS.)

STEVEN: Look at that, Vicki.

(STEVEN *points upwards.* VICKI *shields her eyes with her hand and looks at the sky.)*

VICKI: Three suns!

STEVEN: I wonder which one we're revolving around?

(*As* VICKI *looks away, something in a clump of bushes nearby catches her eye.)*

VICKI: There's the flowers we could smell.

(*She moves across to examine them.)*

They're almost roses, but not quite.

(THE DOCTOR *moves away from the TARDIS, glances up at the suns, then looks around.)*

THE DOCTOR: The silence is just like it was on the planet Xeros.

VICKI: We haven't jumped a time-track again, have we?

THE DOCTOR: No, no, not this time, my child. Yet it's so quiet...

STEVEN: Too quiet.

VICKI: Doctor!

(THE DOCTOR *and* STEVEN *turn. From behind the TARDIS a* CHUMBLEY *appears, pointing a short, rod-like appendage at them, from beneath its dome.)*

STEVEN: It looks dangerous to me. Is that some sort of a gun?

(STEVEN looks around for something to use as a weapon.)

THE DOCTOR: Keep still. Don't do anything! You'll have us killed.

(THE DOCTOR moves cautiously nearer the CHUMBLEY.)

We wish you no harm. We come in peace.

(STEVEN edges slowly to the right as THE DOCTOR speaks.)

VICKI: It can't speak.

THE DOCTOR: No? That thing on the front looks strangely like a speaker to me.

(STEVEN slowly bends to pick up a broken piece of asphalt. As he does he makes a slight sound. Immediately the CHUMBLEY trains its gun on him.)

VICKI: Steven - look out!

THE DOCTOR: You young fool!

STEVEN: I was only trying to...

THE DOCTOR: Yes, yes, yes, very noble of you. Now that

thing is on its guard. Interesting though, did you notice that it didn't know what you were doing until you made a noise?

STEVEN: Then it is blind.

VICKI: But it can hear.

THE DOCTOR: And very accurately at that. It might also be locating us by heat waves, or something of the sort.

(*With its usual chirruping sounds, the* CHUMBLEY *moves towards them. It reaches* THE DOCTOR *and nudges him.* THE DOCTOR *steps back and it nudges him again. He backs some more. The* CHUMBLEY *then moves away and starts to move towards* STEVEN *and* VICKI.)

STEVEN: It's trying to get us to go somewhere.

THE DOCTOR: Indeed. But stand still. Don't let it move you.

(*They remain as they are despite the nudges of the* CHUMBLEY. *Then it pauses, as it apparently receives a message. It chatters to itself, then points its gun at some vegetation on one of the rocky slopes and fires. The vegetation instantly bursts into flame.* THE DOCTOR, VICKI *and* STEVEN *react at this demonstration.*)

Yes. As neat a threat as I ever saw.

VICKI: What was it?

THE DOCTOR: A light ray, I should think. Very powerful
                   and dangerous, whatever it was. We'd bet-
                   ter do what the thing wants.

                   *(The three travellers turn in the direc-
                   tion the* CHUMBLEY *indicates, and they
                   move off. The* CHUMBLEY *follows closely
                   behind. As they move across the land-
                   scape, the* CHUMBLEY *moves from side to
                   side, for all the world like a destroyer
                   herding a convoy into harbour. A short
                   way ahead a spur of rock overhangs the
                   route that they are taking. Two women
                   appear on the spur. They are* DRAHVINS.
                   *They have long blonde hair and have all
                   the assets of femininity, except that none
                   of them are used. They are lacking in
                   any warmth, any expression. Their faces
                   are straight and set, and show no emo-
                   tion. They wear plain green and white,
                   high-necked uniforms. Each holds a
                   futuristic-looking gun. Both look
                   towards the* CHUMBLEY *and the trav-
                   ellers as they approach.* DRAHVIN TWO
                   *puts her gun aside and holds up a thin
                   sheet of metal mesh.* DRAHVIN ONE *also
                   puts her gun aside and grasps the other
                   edge of the mesh sheet. As* THE DOCTOR,
                   STEVEN *and* VICKI *approach, the*
                   DRAHVINS *ease themselves forward in
                   readiness. Together the two* DRAHVINS

hurl the mesh down, and it lands on the
CHUMBLEY. *The* CHUMBLEY'*s domes
instantly collapse down on top of each
other.* THE DOCTOR, VICKI *and* STEVEN
turn in surprise.)

What the...

(DRAHVIN ONE *stays above on the rock
spur, but* DRAHVIN TWO *moves down to
join the travellers.*)

VICKI:	Who are they?
STEVEN:	I couldn't say, but they're a lovely surprise.
DRAHVIN ONE:	We are the Drahvin.
STEVEN:	And very nice too.
THE DOCTOR:	What might the Drahvin be?
DRAHVIN ONE:	We are from the Planet Drahva, in Galaxy 4.
STEVEN:	You've certainly put this thing out of action.
DRAHVIN ONE:	For as long as it is covered in this metal mesh the control waves can't reach it.
VICKI:	What do you want?
DRAHVIN TWO:	We came to rescue you from the machines.
STEVEN:	Why?

DRAHVIN TWO: Maaga will tell you.

STEVEN: Maaga?

DRAHVIN ONE: Our leader.

THE DOCTOR: Why can't you tell us?

DRAHVIN ONE: Our mission was to rescue you. We have done that. We have no other instructions, except to take you to Maaga.

DRAHVIN TWO: We do nothing until a leader speaks.

THE DOCTOR: I see.

DRAHVIN TWO: You will come now.

(VICKI *whispers to* THE DOCTOR.)

VICKI: Doctor, I don't trust them.

DRAHVIN ONE: If you stay here more machines will come and you will be captured and taken to the Rills.

THE DOCTOR: The Rills? Are they the people who control these?

DRAHVIN TWO: They are not people.

DRAHVIN ONE: They are things.

DRAHVIN TWO: They crawl.

DRAHVIN ONE: They murder.

VICKI: Murder?

DRAHVIN TWO: They have already killed one of us.

THE DOCTOR:	I'd like to see these Rills.
STEVEN:	And be killed?
THE DOCTOR:	That's only what they say. And who are they?
STEVEN:	At least they stopped the Chumbley. Doesn't that prove something?
THE DOCTOR:	All right. Take us to... Maaga, or whatever it was you called your leader.

(VICKI suddenly spins round and grabs at THE DOCTOR's arm as she points.)

VICKI:	Doctor! Chumblies!

(They all turn. In the distance several CHUMBLIES are moving in a straight line towards them.)

DRAHVIN ONE:	The mesh.

(The two DRAHVINS try to remove the mesh sheet from the CHUMBLEY, but it will not come off. The others watch.)

It's caught.

THE DOCTOR:	Or the Chumbley is magnetised to make sure you can't get it off.
VICKI:	Doctor, they are getting very close.

(THE DOCTOR looks round and reacts.)

THE DOCTOR:	Goodness me, so they are.

STEVEN: We'll be caught again.

(He turns to the two DRAHVINS.*)*

It isn't coming off.

DRAHVIN TWO: We were instructed not to leave it.

STEVEN: Were you instructed to be killed as well?

DRAHVIN ONE: We must go. Come.

VICKI: They're nearly here.

(They move off. A moment later the pursuing CHUMBLIES *move in and circle the other* CHUMBLEY *trapped beneath the metal mesh. One* CHUMBLEY *moves in and reaches out to grasp the metal mesh with its mechanical arm. It pulls the mesh clear, releasing its trapped companion. They move off in the same direction that the* DRAHVINS, THE DOCTOR *and his companions have taken.)*

14. EXTERIOR DRAHVIN SPACESHIP.

*(*THE DOCTOR, VICKI *and* STEVEN *and the two* DRAHVINS *approach the door of the spaceship. All of them are out of breath from running and clearly exhausted.)*

THE DOCTOR: Oh, my word. Oh dear, dear.

VICKI: Are you all right, Doctor?

THE DOCTOR: I think so. Yes, just I'm not very good at physical exercise these days.

(DRAHVIN ONE *looks back nervously in the direction from which they have come.*)

DRAHVIN ONE: They're nearly here. Quickly. Inside.

(DRAHVIN ONE *leads and the others follow her into the spaceship.*)

15. INTERIOR SPACESHIP AIRLOCK.

DRAHVIN ONE: Close external door.

DRAHVIN THREE *(oov)*: Close external door.

(*The door they have just come through slides shut, with a whine of power. The door has a large window in it.* VICKI *looks through it, as* THE DOCTOR *and* STEVEN *study their surroundings.*)

STEVEN: It's pretty big.

THE DOCTOR: Yes, yes... and more than a little backward. Mmm... primitive stuff.

VICKI: We only just beat the Chumblies. They're out there now.

THE DOCTOR: Are we safe in here?

DRAHVIN ONE: Yes, they cannot enter.

DRAHVIN TWO: Silence! Maaga is coming.

THE DOCTOR: Oh, so it's Maaga again.

(*The interior door slides open, and they are led into the spaceship.*)

16. *INTERIOR DRAHVIN SPACESHIP.*

MAAGA: Report.

DRAHVIN ONE: Mission accomplished. We have brought the prisoners.

VICKI: Prisoners?

MAAGA: And the mesh sheet?

DRAHVIN ONE: It stopped the machine.

MAAGA: Good.

DRAHVIN ONE: We could not get the mesh back again.

MAAGA: What?

DRAHVIN ONE: It became affixed to the machine.

(STEVEN *whispers to* THE DOCTOR.)

STEVEN: She's got them pretty frightened, hasn't she?

THE DOCTOR: It's quite true what the young lady says. I think you'll find it was magnetised.

(MAAGA *glances at* THE DOCTOR, *then back to the two* DRAHVINS.)

MAAGA:	I will deal with you both later. Sit.
	(DRAHVIN ONE *and* DRAHVIN TWO *go to a bench and sit down.* MAAGA *looks across at* THE DOCTOR, STEVEN *and* VICKI, *and attempts to soften her voice.*)
	I'm sorry to have kept you waiting. Sit down.
THE DOCTOR:	Thank you, yes.
MAAGA:	I have to hear the reports first.
THE DOCTOR:	Yes, naturally, of course.
MAAGA:	It is necessary when you are at war.
STEVEN:	At war?
MAAGA:	With the Rills, and their machines.
VICKI:	Chumblies.
MAAGA:	This is a fight to the death. For existence itself...
	(THE DOCTOR *nods to himself, thinking, but gives no other reaction.*)
THE DOCTOR:	Oh, I see.
MAAGA:	...in which one of us will be obliterated.
THE DOCTOR:	As bad as that?
MAAGA:	Yes. Very bad indeed. So bad that it is conceivable that you too will be obliterated.

THE DOCTOR: Oh, come, come... there's no need to exaggerate.

MAAGA: There's no exaggeration.

VICKI: You want to kill us, don't you? You do.

MAAGA: When a planet disintegrates, nothing survives.

(THE DOCTOR *is suddenly alert, his first real reaction.*)

THE DOCTOR: Disintegrates? This planet?

MAAGA: This one. It is in its last moments of life... soon it will explode.

THE DOCTOR: When?

MAAGA: In fourteen dawns time.

STEVEN: How do you know? How can you be so certain?

MAAGA: The Rills told us. That is why they are repairing their space machine. So they can escape.

THE DOCTOR: Yes, well that seems reasonable.

MAAGA: We must capture their spaceship from them.

STEVEN: Why? This is a spaceship, isn't it?

MAAGA: But it will not fly. The Rills shot us down. We cannot move.

STEVEN: You don't belong here?

MAAGA: No. Nor do the Rills. There is no life on this planet. We come from Drahva. Four hundred dawns ago we were investigating this section of the galaxy. We were seeking a planet like this, capable of supporting life, so that we could colonise it. There are too many of us on Drahva.

STEVEN: All women?

MAAGA: Women?

STEVEN: Yes, you know... er...

THE DOCTOR: Feminine. Female.

MAAGA: We have a small number of men, as many as we need. The rest we killed. They consumed valuable food and served no particular purpose.

(MAAGA *gestures disdainfully at the two* DRAHVINS.)

And these are not what you would call... human. They are cultivated, in test tubes. We have very good scientists.

(THE DOCTOR *gives a non-committal grunt.*)

I am a living being. They are... products. And inferior at that. Grown for a purpose, and capable of nothing more.

STEVEN: And the purpose?

MAAGA: To fight. To kill.

THE DOCTOR: What an interesting civilisation yours must be. I take it you attacked the Rills.

MAAGA: We were in space above this planet when we saw a ship such as we had never seen before. We didn't know it, but it was the Rills' ship. It fired on us, we crashed. But before we did we succeeded in firing back so that their ship crashed as well. They managed to kill one of my soldiers.

STEVEN: What do they look like, these Rills?

MAAGA: Disgusting.

THE DOCTOR: That's no description. No description at all.

MAAGA: It's all I will say.

THE DOCTOR: But now I begin to understand.

STEVEN: So do I. This planet is going to explode and they've managed to build a ship to get off in time. You haven't, so you want theirs.

MAAGA: We do not wish to be here when this planet ceases to exist.

DRAHVIN   Machine approaching.
THREE (oov):

17. EXTERIOR.

(A CHUMBLEY *moves across the land-scape, approaching the* DRAHVINS' *spaceship.)*

18. INTERIOR DRAHVIN SPACESHIP.

*(*DRAHVIN THREE *comes through a com-municating door.* MAAGA *strides to an observation window and looks out.)*

MAAGA: Your stations.

(Immediately the DRAHVINS *take up posi-tions by projections in the bulkhead, which are in fact guns.)*

Switch off the outside radio.

(One of the DRAHVINS *operates a switch.)*

VICKI: What are they going to do?

STEVEN: Try again at the Chumblies, by the look of it.

THE DOCTOR: Hmm. But why switch off the outside radio, I wonder?

*(*MAAGA *turns from the observation win-dow to answer.)*

MAAGA: They send the machines to tell us lies. We do not want to hear them.

THE DOCTOR: Perhaps you don't, but I'd like to.

MAAGA: It is not good for my soldiers.

(THE DOCTOR *goes over to the observation window.*)

THE DOCTOR: I see. It's stopped.

MAAGA: Yes. It will be speaking its message now... Fire!

(*There is a hissing noise as the guns are discharged.*)

19. EXTERIOR.

(*The* CHUMBLEY *is hit by a burst of smoke and flame. It collapses its domes and is still for a moment, then it raises them again, chatters to itself, as if sending a message, and turns and chumbles off.*)

20. INTERIOR DRAHVIN SPACESHIP.

(THE DOCTOR *and* MAAGA *are looking out of the observation window.*)

THE DOCTOR: Well, you didn't do him much damage, did you?

MAAGA: My only intention was to drive it off. We have succeeded.

(She turns to address the other DRAHVINS.*)*

Back to your places.

*(*DRAHVIN ONE *and* DRAHVIN TWO *immediately go back to the bench.* DRAHVIN THREE *exits.)*

THE DOCTOR: You haven't destroyed a single Chumbley yet, have you?

MAAGA: We will.

THE DOCTOR: I think you underestimate the Rills. And why should they tell you that this planet is about to die?

MAAGA: They were trying to tempt us to their ship so that they could kill us.

STEVEN: They offered to help you?

MAAGA: That is what they claimed.

VICKI: But they might have been telling the truth. They might have meant it.

THE DOCTOR: Yes... it might have all been lies, too.

MAAGA: What do you mean?

THE DOCTOR: Well, this planet might last for another billion years.

MAAGA: We have no way of checking that.

THE DOCTOR: Ah, but I have. I am a scientist.

(MAAGA *stares at* THE DOCTOR.)

MAAGA: Very well. I would be grateful if you would find out.

THE DOCTOR: Then I'll have to go back to my ship. If you'll excuse us.

(THE DOCTOR *moves to the door and indicates for* VICKI *and* STEVEN *to join him.*)

MAAGA: Wait. You cannot all go.

THE DOCTOR: Oh. Why not?

VICKI: Prisoners, are we?

MAAGA: Of course not. But if you encounter the machines...

STEVEN: What of it?

MAAGA: We could not guarantee to rescue again.

THE DOCTOR: Oh, you worry too much.

MAAGA: I would feel easier if one of you remained here.

VICKI: I'll stay.

THE DOCTOR: But, my dear...

VICKI: I'll stay. You'll need Steven if you run into the Chumblies.

THE DOCTOR: Very well, we'll go alone. Young man...

(MAAGA *signals for* DRAHVIN TWO *to open the door and airlock. As* THE DOCTOR *and* STEVEN *leave,* STEVEN *turns to* VICKI *and gives her a reassuring smile.*)

STEVEN: We won't be long, Vicki. I promise not to get lost.

(VICKI *nods and smiles bravely.* STEVEN *exits after* THE DOCTOR.)

21. EXTERIOR.

(THE DOCTOR *and* STEVEN *appear over the edge of a slope.* THE DOCTOR *grabs at* STEVEN *warning him to take cover.*)

THE DOCTOR: Wait!

(They both crouch down and look ahead. A CHUMBLEY *is by the* TARDIS *and is making obvious attempts to gain entry. After a little while it gives up and withdraws, to be replaced immediately by a second* CHUMBLEY, *who moves up to the ship. There is a screaming of metal as it brings some mechanised force to bear against the door.* THE DOCTOR *and* STEVEN *continue to watch from their vantage point.)*

STEVEN: Can they get in?

THE DOCTOR: I shouldn't think so.

STEVEN: But you don't know?

THE DOCTOR: They'd have to be extremely advanced to break my force barrier.

STEVEN: How do you know they aren't?

(THE DOCTOR *doesn't answer, but is clearly not too concerned.*)

22. *INTERIOR DRAHVIN SPACESHIP.*

(VICKI *is on her own in the spaceship. She sits on a bench, tense and unhappy. She sighs, stands up, and is about to move to look out of the observation window when she hears something. She goes over to the wall and presses her ear against it.*)

MAAGA *(oov)*:   To lose the mesh was gross incompetence. It was our only weapon against the machines. If we lose to the Rills, it will be because of you. You want that, do you? You want to be captured by those creeping, revolting green monsters? You want their slimy claws to close about your necks?

(VICKI *hears the* DRAHVINS *moan in terror.*)

You fools! You fools!

(*Horrified,* VICKI *shrinks away.*)

23. EXTERIOR.

(A CHUMBLEY, *in a last futile attempt, tries his light ray on the doors of the TARDIS. The* CHUMBLEY *gives up, transmits a message and chumbles off. As soon as it has gone,* THE DOCTOR *and* STEVEN *appear.* THE DOCTOR *examines the TARDIS door.)*

THE DOCTOR: Look at that, my boy. Not a scratch. My word, I excelled myself with that force field, I really did.

STEVEN: Are we going inside, or not?

THE DOCTOR: What? Oh, yes, yes, yes.

(He takes out his key and opens the door.)

Good job you're here to remind me what I'm supposed to be doing, eh?

STEVEN: You're so right, Doctor.

(They enter the TARDIS.)

24. INTERIOR THE TARDIS.

*(*THE DOCTOR *moves across to his astral map machine and presses buttons. Lights come on and he adjusts various dials, with great pleasure.)*

THE DOCTOR: There. Mmm... let's see.

(There is a flickering of light and THE DOCTOR *closely watches the screen.)*

STEVEN: Well, Doctor? Will this planet explode?

*(*THE DOCTOR *nods, coming to a decision.)*

THE DOCTOR: Yes, yes it will. The Rills were quite right.

STEVEN: Then we must get off this planet immediately.

THE DOCTOR: And you think the Drahvins will let us?

STEVEN: Why shouldn't they?

THE DOCTOR: Because they want our help against the Rills. Why do you think they kept Vicki back? Do you think they were worried about her health?

STEVEN: But we must get off somehow.

THE DOCTOR: Yes, my boy, we must. And quickly.

STEVEN: Why the rush, Doctor? The Drahvins did say fourteen dawns.

THE DOCTOR: Two dawns. Tomorrow is the last day this planet will see!

Next Episode :
TRAP OF STEEL

EPISODE TWO

TRAP OF STEEL

1. INTERIOR THE TARDIS (DAY).

STEVEN: But we must get off somehow.

THE DOCTOR: Yes, my boy, we must. And quickly.

STEVEN: Why the rush, Doctor? The Drahvins did say fourteen dawns.

THE DOCTOR: Two dawns. Tomorrow is the last day this planet will see!

2. INTERIOR DRAHVIN SPACESHIP.

(VICKI is alone. She goes over to the observation window and looks out.)

3. INTERIOR THE TARDIS.

STEVEN: We must get Vicki away from the Drahvins.

(He crosses over to THE DOCTOR.)

Let's have a look on the scanner, Doctor.

(THE DOCTOR *operates the scanner. A*
CHUMBLEY *is moving towards the*
TARDIS, carrying a black phial-shaped
object supported on two wires.)

4. *EXTERIOR.*

STEVEN *(oov)*: What's that it's got?

THE DOCTOR
(oov):
I wish I knew.

(*The* CHUMBLEY *moves right in, bumping*
into the side of the police box, then
drops the phial. The CHUMBLEY *chatters,*
turns about and moves off. As it does so,
two wires can be seen in its grip, run-
ning back to the phial. The CHUMBLEY
moves away to a safe distance, turns to
face the TARDIS and halts, holding the
ends of the wires a few inches apart.)

STEVEN *(oov)*: Perhaps it's just going to stand guard
there.

THE DOCTOR
(oov):
No, no, it's waiting for something.

STEVEN *(oov)*: But what?

THE DOCTOR
(oov):
I can't quite see.

5. *INTERIOR THE TARDIS.*

STEVEN: I think it's... yes, it's holding two wires. Doctor...

(There is a loud explosion and the TARDIS shakes, and then is still again. STEVEN gets up and shakes his head to clear it.)

Doctor? Doctor?

(THE DOCTOR sits up from behind the control console. STEVEN goes over and helps THE DOCTOR to his feet.)

Are you all right?

THE DOCTOR: Goodness me, whatever will they try next?

STEVEN: Do you think it's done any damage?

THE DOCTOR: What? No, no. It will take more than that to get in here, I assure you.

(There is a bumping and sliding sound from outside.)

STEVEN: He's come to investigate.

THE DOCTOR: Then he'll be disappointed.

(They move across to the scanner. THE DOCTOR nods to himself and motions towards the screen.)

There he goes, look. Off into the distance,

empty-handed.

STEVEN: Given up.

THE DOCTOR: Yes, or to come back with some other piece of trouble. Right, off we go. We haven't got a lot of time left.

STEVEN: Two dawns... no time at all.

(THE DOCTOR *operates the door control and they exit.*)

6. *INTERIOR DRAHVIN SPACESHIP.*

(MAAGA *sits at a table, eating.*)

MAAGA: You're sure you won't eat?

VICKI: No, thank you.

MAAGA: It's good.

(VICKI *looks in disgust at what* MAAGA *is eating.*)

VICKI: It looks like leaves to me.

MAAGA: It is leaves.

VICKI: Is that what you eat?

MAAGA: Of course.

VICKI: Ugh!

MAAGA: Everything that lives must eat. This is...

(VICKI *interrupts and stands up.*)

VICKI: They've been gone ages. It must be at least two hours.

MAAGA: They will be back.

VICKI: Perhaps a Chumbley caught them.

MAAGA: No, they wouldn't let themselves be caught. They would be too worried about you.

VICKI: That's why you kept me here, isn't it?

(MAAGA *continues eating and does not reply.*)

Isn't it?

MAAGA: You are safe here.

VICKI: Safe!

MAAGA: Exactly.

VICKI: Can't I go and look for them?

MAAGA: If they are not back soon, we shall go and look.

VICKI: Please, let me.

MAAGA: If I did that, you might all escape in your ship. And we need your help.

VICKI: I see. Whether we want to give it or not.

(MAAGA *gives a very unpleasant smile.*)

MAAGA: I am sure that all of you want to help us.

7. *EXTERIOR DRAHVIN SPACESHIP.*

(THE DOCTOR *and* STEVEN *approach the spaceship.*)

STEVEN: Made it.

(THE DOCTOR *nods, his attention on the spaceship.* STEVEN *follows his gaze.*)

You know, this is a strange kind of space-ship.

THE DOCTOR: Not a very good one, either. Not advanced at all, in fact it's old-fashioned. They aren't very intelligent, these Drahvins. And that reminds me...

(THE DOCTOR *starts to search through his pockets.*)

STEVEN: What now?

THE DOCTOR: Oh, just curious.

(*He brings out a small screwdriver.*)

Ah, there it is. Thought I'd lost it.

STEVEN: What do you want it for?

THE DOCTOR: As I said, my boy, mere curiosity.

(He approaches the ship, scratches the metal hull with the screwdriver and peers at the metal.)

Tough, but not impregnable. A reasonably common metal... nothing special about it, nothing special at all.

(As THE DOCTOR *thinks to himself,* STEVEN *watches in puzzlement.* THE DOC-TOR *suddenly turns to him.)*

Well, let's go in, my boy. Don't hang about there admiring the scenery.

STEVEN: It was you...

THE DOCTOR: Now, don't argue. Don't argue.

(They go inside the airlock.)

8. INTERIOR DRAHVIN SPACESHIP.

*(*VICKI *turns expectantly towards the entrance.)*

MAAGA: Your friends. Safe, you see.

VICKI: No thanks to you though, is it?

*(*THE DOCTOR *and* STEVEN *enter.* VICKI *runs over to them.)*

Are you all right, Doctor?

THE DOCTOR: Yes, yes, quite all right, my child.

VICKI: Only you were such a long time.

STEVEN: Well, we'd have been a lot quicker if it hadn't been for the Doctor fiddling...

THE DOCTOR: Eh?!

STEVEN: We were held up by a Chumbley.

THE DOCTOR: Yes, and it tried to blow up the TARDIS while we were in it!

MAAGA: He did not succeed?

THE DOCTOR: Well of course he didn't. My ship isn't a piece of old tin like this, you know. Seems to me this thing of yours would fall apart if I coughed too loudly.

MAAGA: It serves its purpose.

THE DOCTOR: More than likely.

> (MAAGA *pulls a lever on the wall and the door shuts.*)

Is that necessary?

MAAGA: We have to protect ourselves against the machines... Did you find out about this planet?

THE DOCTOR: Yes...

MAAGA: It will explode?

THE DOCTOR: Yes... yes, I'm afraid so.

MAAGA: When?

THE DOCTOR: Exactly when the Rills said. In fourteen dawns.

  (STEVEN *goes to speak, then decides against it.*)

MAAGA: Fourteen dawns.

VICKI: Well, we should prepare to go, shouldn't we? We ought to...

  (VICKI *falls silent.* THE DOCTOR *sits down at the table.*)

MAAGA: Doctor?

THE DOCTOR: Yes?

MAAGA: Will you help us?

THE DOCTOR: To do what, exactly?

MAAGA: To capture the Rills' spaceship so that we can escape.

THE DOCTOR: And how do I do that, hmm? What happens then?

MAAGA: What do you mean?

THE DOCTOR: I mean the Rills. What happens to the Rills?

MAAGA: They stay on the planet.

VICKI: To be blown up?

MAAGA: They are murderers.

STEVEN: Why couldn't you take them off with you?

MAAGA: Because they are evil. You have only to see them to know that. Evil.

THE DOCTOR: We have only your word for that. But in any case, I can't do it.

MAAGA: Oh?

THE DOCTOR: In the first place, I kill nothing. Nor do my friends.

MAAGA: Either the Rills die or we do.

THE DOCTOR: Or as my young friend says, you both get off together.

MAAGA: Impossible.

STEVEN: What's so impossible about it? Have you ever tried being friendly?

THE DOCTOR: A good question.

VICKI: It sounds to me as if you want to be enemies.

MAAGA: The situation was forced upon us.

STEVEN: Maybe they killed your soldier by mistake?

MAAGA: There was no mistake about it.

STEVEN: You seem very sure for someone who was knocked unconscious by the crash.

MAAGA: You, too, doubt my word?

VICKI: Seems to me we'd be silly not to.

THE DOCTOR: And all of these objections sum up mine.
              This is not our business. Not our business
              at all. We don't know you, and we don't
              know the Rills either. No, no, impossible.
              We can't help you, and it doesn't even
              look to me as though you've tried to help
              yourselves.

STEVEN: Too busy fighting.

MAAGA: Then you will not help?

THE DOCTOR: No.

              (MAAGA *produces a hand weapon from
              her belt. She points it at* THE DOCTOR.)

MAAGA: You will not change your mind?

THE DOCTOR: No.

MAAGA: This is your last chance.

THE DOCTOR: Very likely.

MAAGA: Possibly you don't realise it, but if first I
              point this at your hand, then press the...

              (*From the first moment when she drew
              the gun,* STEVEN *has been judging his
              distance. Suddenly, he leaps and grabs
              the gun with both hands, forcing it
              upwards. They sway to and fro whilst*

VICKI *and* THE DOCTOR *watch in conster-*
nation. Although MAAGA *does not look*
as though she possesses great strength,
she is certainly much stronger than
STEVEN *expects and he is forced back.)*

9. EXTERIOR DRAHVIN SPACESHIP.

(The three DRAHVINS, *who have been on*
patrol, move towards the spaceship and
into the airlock, looking around to make
sure there are no CHUMBLIES.)

10. INTERIOR DRAHVIN SPACESHIP.

(As the DRAHVINS *enter the room, they*
see MAAGA *and* STEVEN *struggling and*
immediately draw their guns. VICKI
shouts a warning to STEVEN.)

VICKI: Steven!

*(*STEVEN *sees the guns and gives up the*
struggle with MAAGA.)

THE DOCTOR: Never mind, my boy. A good attempt.

MAAGA: You will help us now?

THE DOCTOR: We don't seem to have much choice.

MAAGA: You have none at all. The Rills are repairing their spaceship. They have fourteen
dawns in which to complete it.

(STEVEN *and* THE DOCTOR *glance at each other, which does not go unnoticed by* MAAGA.)

It is fourteen, isn't it?

THE DOCTOR: Mmm. Oh yes, of course it is.

MAAGA: You are sure?

THE DOCTOR: Quite sure.

MAAGA: Suddenly I don't believe you.

THE DOCTOR: Why should I lie?

MAAGA: To try to trick us, somehow. When is the planet due to explode?

THE DOCTOR: In fourteen dawns.

(MAAGA *nods her head and two of the* DRAHVINS *seize* VICKI. *The third points her gun at* VICKI.)

MAAGA: Very well. We shall kill the girl.

THE DOCTOR: Two dawns.

(MAAGA *is clearly shocked.*)

MAAGA: As soon as that?

THE DOCTOR: Yes.

MAAGA: You must move quickly. Their spaceship is that way.

(*She points into the distance.*)

	You will capture it for us.
THE DOCTOR:	And how do I do that, mmm?
MAAGA:	That is your problem. But you still have one advantage. The Rills still think they have fourteen dawns. We know otherwise, don't we?
THE DOCTOR:	Their ship may not be ready.
STEVEN:	If it were, they'd take off now.
MAAGA:	I'm sure the Doctor could attend to that too.
THE DOCTOR:	You seem to have a great amount of faith in me.
MAAGA:	Because I shall keep one of you here. I shall keep the girl.
STEVEN:	No you won't. You'll keep me.
MAAGA:	I said the girl.
STEVEN:	Do you want our help, or don't you?
MAAGA:	Yes, of course we do.
THE DOCTOR:	Then you'll do as the young man says.
MAAGA:	All right. We keep him.
THE DOCTOR:	Come along, Vicki. We don't have much time.

(VICKI *follows* THE DOCTOR, *who gives an*

appreciative nod to STEVEN. THE DOCTOR
*reaches the closed airlock door and taps
it with his stick.)*

Am I supposed to start by walking
through this?

*(*MAAGA *presses the switch and the door
slides open.* THE DOCTOR *and* VICKI *look
at* STEVEN *again, and then leave.)*

STEVEN: Do you really think they'll be able to capture the Rills' spaceship?

MAAGA: If they don't we shall all die together.

*11. EXTERIOR DRAHVIN SPACESHIP
(EVENING).*

*(*THE DOCTOR *and* VICKI *are outside the*
DRAHVIN *spaceship.* THE DOCTOR *gazes
up at the sky, deep in thought.)*

VICKI: What is it, Doctor?

THE DOCTOR: What? Oh, I've been wondering why it
hasn't got dark. But of course, this planet
has three suns.

VICKI: You don't think they have night here then?

THE DOCTOR: They must do, otherwise that Maaga
woman wouldn't talk about dawns. Probably only lasts a couple of hours though.

(As THE DOCTOR *moves off, his eyes wan-*

der to where he scratched the spaceship wall with his screwdriver. VICKI *follows his gaze, sees the mark and crosses to it.* THE DOCTOR *comes back to join her.)*

Do you remember when we were captured by that Chumbley?

VICKI: Yes, of course.

THE DOCTOR: That gun it had... a light ray. Why don't they use it on this ship? I mean... if the Rills are such enemies of the Drahvins, why don't they just wipe them out?

VICKI: Perhaps the rays can't cut through metal?

THE DOCTOR: Oh, they could. Believe me, that ray could cut through this as though it were paper.

VICKI: But they have not even tried by the look of it.

THE DOCTOR: There's not a mark, except for the one I made. Odd. Very odd.

VICKI: Doctor, we haven't got much time.

THE DOCTOR: It's very nearly one dawn. We'd better start our journey.

(VICKI *shudders as she recalls the* DRAHVIN's *description of the* RILLS.)

VICKI: Oh... they do sound horrid.

12. INTERIOR DRAHVIN SPACESHIP.

(STEVEN goes over to DRAHVIN TWO and touches her gun. He then walks over to DRAHVIN ONE and takes her gun. To his surprise he realises that both the guns are non-functional. He gives it back to her.)

STEVEN: It won't work, but it looks pretty. Can I have some food?

(DRAHVIN ONE offers him a plate, with twigs and leaves on it.)

Is that all there is?

DRAHVIN ONE: That is our food.

STEVEN: Maaga eats this?

DRAHVIN ONE: No, she is our leader.

STEVEN: Then I'll try what she eats.

DRAHVIN ONE: You cannot. That is food for our leaders only.

STEVEN: That doesn't seem very fair, does it?

DRAHVIN ONE: Fair?

STEVEN: Well, that she should have special food while you have to eat this.

DRAHVIN ONE: It is food.

STEVEN: Does Maaga have other 'special' things.

DRAHVIN ONE: She is our leader and has leader's things.

STEVEN: What leader's things?

DRAHVIN ONE: Her gun, her food, her...

STEVEN: Her gun?

DRAHVIN ONE: A leader's gun can destroy anything.

STEVEN: Even the Chumblies?

DRAHVIN ONE: Even the machines.

STEVEN: Then surely it would be better if you all had these guns. Then you wouldn't have to fear the machines.

DRAHVIN ONE: There is only one. Maaga has it as she is the leader.

STEVEN: You could use it when you went out on patrol though.

DRAHVIN ONE: Yes.

STEVEN: Then doesn't it seem right that you should?

DRAHVIN ONE: Only if Maaga says so.

STEVEN: If you took it and went out against the machines and destroyed one, then Maaga would be pleased with you.

(DRAHVIN ONE *does not react.*)

She would be pleased if you destroyed a machine.

DRAHVIN ONE: Yes.

STEVEN: Then you should take her gun.

DRAHVIN ONE: Yes.

STEVEN: Give me your gun while you go and get Maaga's gun, then we will destroy the machines together.

DRAHVIN ONE: Yes.

(*Without being noticed,* MAAGA *has entered the room.*)

MAAGA: You are trying to be too clever.

(*She reprimands* DRAHVIN ONE.)

You have done badly... you will be punished. This is a prisoner. You must not talk to him.

DRAHVIN ONE: He was talking.

MAAGA: He was trying to trick you, like the machines.

DRAHVIN ONE: I was wrong. I did not understand.

MAAGA: Go to your quarters.

(DRAHVIN ONE *exits.* MAAGA *turns back to* STEVEN.)

You will have to keep out of our way.

STEVEN: I don't particularly want to be here at all.

MAAGA: You don't have to be.

STEVEN: Oh?

MAAGA: You could easily escape from this planet.

STEVEN: Could I?

MAAGA: In your own ship.

STEVEN: Taking you as well?

MAAGA: You would not expect us to stay here.

STEVEN: I suppose not.

MAAGA: Simply take us off this planet and you are free.

STEVEN: Just like that?

MAAGA: It is a fair offer.

STEVEN: Even assuming that I believed you, that you didn't decide along the way that I was eating too much food, there is a snag.

MAAGA: And what is that?

STEVEN: I can't operate it... couldn't even if I tried. Only the Doctor can do that. It's his ship. Why don't you make your offer to him? Or is it that you think he might be too smart for you? I'm the gullible one, am I? Not much help, am I?

MAAGA: I could make you help us.

STEVEN: No, you couldn't. Even I can't do the impossible. Sorry.

*(*MAAGA *glares at him in frustrated rage, then points at a padded area of the room, in one corner.)*

MAAGA: Get over there, and stay there.

STEVEN: That's an order, isn't it?

MAAGA: It is.

(With a last contemptuous stare at MAAGA, STEVEN *permits himself to be shepherded to the corner. He first sits, then lies down, but only after taking another look at the* DRAHVINS, *who are sitting at the table. There is silence. The silence of those who dare not speak. After a while,* DRAHVIN THREE *nervously asks a question.)*

DRAHVIN THREE: Maaga?

MAAGA: What is it?

DRAHVIN THREE: Why do we not kill him now?

MAAGA: I will let you kill him... when I am ready.

*(*STEVEN *overhears this remark.)*

13. EXTERIOR.

(THE DOCTOR *and* VICKI *are lying down looking over a ledge several feet high. The noise of the* CHUMBLIES *can be heard nearby, and the* RILLS' *spaceship is obviously close at hand. As they watch, a* CHUMBLEY *moves along the ground below them.* THE DOCTOR *and* VICKI *both draw back instinctively. The* CHUMBLEY *goes past and out of sight.*)

VICKI: We'll never get past the sentries.

THE DOCTOR: Fascinating to watch, aren't they? I wonder what the operating principal is. Relatively simple, I should think, once you know it.

VICKI: Doctor!

THE DOCTOR: Yes? Hmm?

VICKI: How are we going to get past the sentries?

THE DOCTOR: Oh, that. It's a problem, I'll admit.

VICKI: It certainly is.

THE DOCTOR: Be patient, child. In this case we must observe, note, collate, then conclude. Then we can act.

VICKI: With the amount of time we've got to spare you'll have to do all that in about ten minutes.

(*Another* CHUMBLEY *approaches.*)

THE DOCTOR: Quiet, child.

(*As it moves past,* VICKI *gets an idea. She gives a sideways glance at* THE DOCTOR *and decides to act. She picks up a rock, weighs it in her hand and hides it from* THE DOCTOR. *The* CHUMBLEY *moves closer.* VICKI *licks her lips and raises the rock.* THE DOCTOR *is giving all his attention to the* CHUMBLEY, *watching it through narrowed eyes. The* CHUMBLEY *moves beneath them and* VICKI *suddenly throws the rock down behind it. It does not react and continues on its course.*)

What the... what the...?

VICKI: That's the answer, Doctor. I thought it might be.

THE DOCTOR: You could have got us both killed.

VICKI: But it only picks up things in front of it, didn't you see? Just so long as we keep behind them, they won't know we're here.

(THE DOCTOR *grudgingly agrees.*)

THE DOCTOR: Yes, yes, it appears you are right... but it was still a very foolish chance to take.

VICKI: It wasn't a chance. I noted, observed, collated, concluded, and all that, just like you said.

(She smiles wickedly.)

Then I threw a rock.

(THE DOCTOR gives her a look and smiles in spite of himself.)

THE DOCTOR: I'll give you the benefit of the doubt. Well, we're going to have to run for it.

(He gets up.)

VICKI: You will be able to manage won't you, Doctor?

THE DOCTOR: I dare say I can manage to drag my aged limbs into something resembling a run.

VICKI: Come on then.

(THE DOCTOR and VICKI run across the landscape, running and dodging, making sure they are behind any CHUMBLIES.)

14. INTERIOR DRAHVIN SPACESHIP.

(The DRAHVINS are still seated at the table, but each one now rigidly holds her gun in front of her. MAAGA is before them. STEVEN is in the background.)

MAAGA: Power units.

(The DRAHVINS *clap their hands to the power units of their guns.)*

Off.

(They click them off.)

Down.

(They put them on the table.)

Guns.

(Their right hands return to the guns.)

Down.

(The guns come down in unison on the table, the DRAHVINS *still rigidly holding them.)*

Power units.

(Their hands move to the power units.)

Readings.

(Each DRAHVIN *looks at the small dial on their gun's power unit.)*

One.

DRAHVIN ONE: Three, nine, seven.

MAAGA: Two.

DRAHVIN TWO: Three, nine, four.

MAAGA: Three.

DRAHVIN
THREE:
Three, eight, six.

MAAGA:
Get it charged, Three.

(DRAHVIN THREE *gets up and goes to the wall. She plugs her gun into a connection, and presses a switch. There is a whine of power.*)

Your guns must be perfect. If I find one defective, its owner will be severely punished.

(*The* DRAHVINS *stare stonily ahead.*)

Because, soon now, they will be used. I, Maaga, will see to it. Very soon now we shall break into the Rill centre.

(*The* DRAHVINS *look at each other and nod meaningfully.*)

And the Rills. They will be wiped out.

(STEVEN *tilts his head slightly and looks at the* DRAHVINS.)

15. *EXTERIOR.*

(THE DOCTOR *and* VICKI *move in and crouch down out of sight.* THE DOCTOR *studies something in front of him, as* VICKI *takes in their surroundings.*)

VICKI: Well, so far, so good.

THE DOCTOR: Yes...

                 (He points.)

                 Well... that's obviously where the Rills...

                 *(VICKI looks in the direction THE DOCTOR
                 is pointing, towards a pillbox-shaped
                 object, made of quarried rock. On the
                 left of it is a vast black sphere. A little to
                 the right and front of the pillbox is what
                 looks like a drill rig.)*

VICKI: And that must be their spaceship on the
                 left.

THE DOCTOR: I wonder what the other thing is.

VICKI: It looks like a... like a drilling rig.

THE DOCTOR: Does, doesn't it? Now what would they be
                 drilling for, hmm?

VICKI: Oil? Gas?

THE DOCTOR: Well, there's only one way to find out.

                 (They get up and move towards it.)

                 16. *EXTERIOR RILL CENTRE.*

                 *(Near a narrow entrance, affixed to the
                 wall, is a piece of machinery of some
                 sort. A* CHUMBLEY *emerges from the*

entrance and comes to rest. Then it swings around and goes back in again. THE DOCTOR *and* VICKI *creep forwards and* THE DOCTOR *examines the wall.)*

VICKI: What if one of them comes out again?

THE DOCTOR: We'd be in trouble. You know Vicki, this is a nice piece of building.

VICKI: Looks very temporary to me.

THE DOCTOR: Quite so, quite so... but nonetheless it's most impressive, most impressive.

(THE DOCTOR moves on and notices the machinery.)

And what's this? Hmm.

(He examines it and clearly draws a conclusion.)

I have to admit these Rills are quite advanced.

(VICKI looks at the machinery.)

VICKI: It's some sort of air purifier.

THE DOCTOR: More than that, I think. Machinery for converting air into something else. Yes... interesting.

(VICKI is peering into the passage. THE DOCTOR *moves to join her.)*

See anything?

(She shakes her head.)

I'll lead the way then.

17. *INTERIOR PASSAGEWAY.*

*(*THE DOCTOR *and* VICKI *pause, looking about themselves.)*

THE DOCTOR: Built for the Chumblies by the look of it.

VICKI: Yes, it's a Chumbley sort of shape.

THE DOCTOR: And if this is for the Rills? Do you smell anything?

*(*VICKI *sniffs and pauses.)*

VICKI: Yes... it's ever so faint though.

THE DOCTOR: What is it?

VICKI: I don't know. But I ought to.

THE DOCTOR: Yes, I thought that too. Well, come on Vicki. This way, I think.

(They move off down the corridor.)

18. *INTERIOR PASSAGEWAY.*

*(*THE DOCTOR *and* VICKI *come into view. They are now deeper inside the* RILL *centre.* THE DOCTOR *pauses to examine*

>   *the wall, running his hand over it.)*

THE DOCTOR: It's very strongly built. Marvellous work.

>   *(VICKI continues on. She stops and turns back to* THE DOCTOR.*)*

VICKI: The smell's getting stronger.

THE DOCTOR: What was that? Oh the smell. Yes...

VICKI: Sssssh!

>   *(They both freeze. They hear an approaching* CHUMBLEY. *The sound grows louder and then fades away again as the* CHUMBLEY *moves off down some other passage.* THE DOCTOR *and* VICKI *relax and, realising the need for silence, signal to each other to move off down the corridor.)*

>   *19. INTERIOR RILL CENTRAL CHAMBER.*

>   *(*THE DOCTOR *and* VICKI *enter a large space and look about them. Here and there, neatly stacked, are various constructional pieces; items of equipment and repair. There are several exits. One wall is black. It is the side of the* RILLS' *spaceship.* THE DOCTOR *sees the black wall.)*

THE DOCTOR: Ah, the spaceship.

(He moves across and examines it.)

Yes, you couldn't scratch this with a screwdriver. A very superior metal. Very superior. Hardly a metal at all in fact. Wonderful material for a spaceship.

VICKI: Doctor?

THE DOCTOR: Yes, what is it?

VICKI: I know what that smell is now.

*(*THE DOCTOR *takes another sniff.)*

It's ammonia.

20. *Exterior Rill Centre.*

(A CHUMBLEY *comes into view, then moves into the passageway and out of sight.)*

21. *Interior Rill Central Chamber.*

*(*THE DOCTOR *and* VICKI *are still examining the chamber.)*

VICKI: What do you think this space is for, Doctor?

THE DOCTOR: Looks like some sort of repair shop to me. See?

(He points.)

Attachments for the Chumblies.

(VICKI *notices a deactivated* CHUMBLEY, *its domes collapsed together, making it look smaller than the others.*)

VICKI: Doctor, look... do you think it's a baby one?

THE DOCTOR: I don't think it's awake yet. The ammonia smell's not so strong here.

(VICKI *turns, her eyes reacting in horror to what she sees. She screams.*)

VICKI: Doctor, look!

Next Episode:
AIR LOCK

EPISODE THREE

AIR LOCK

1. INTERIOR RILL CENTRAL CHAMBER.

(VICKI turns, her eyes reacting in horror to what she sees. She screams.)

VICKI: Doctor, look!

(THE DOCTOR turns and looks. He is also rivetted by what he sees. In the middle of a door that they had not previously noticed is a window, and beyond the window, in a cloud of swirling ammonia, are two large scaly eyes, staring out at them.)

2. INTERIOR PASSAGEWAY.

(A CHUMBLEY moves along. It reaches the end of the passageway and moves off into another.)

3. *INTERIOR RILL CENTRAL CHAMBER.*

(THE DOCTOR *and* VICKI *turn as they hear the sound of a* CHUMBLEY *approaching.*)

THE DOCTOR: A Chumbley! Quick, child.

(*They both rush towards one of the passageways and pull to a halt as they see a* CHUMBLEY *coming towards them. They turn and flee down another passageway. The noise of the* CHUMBLIES *loud in their ears.*)

4. *INTERIOR PASSAGEWAY.*

(THE DOCTOR *and* VICKI *hurry along, the sound of pursuing* CHUMBLIES *not far behind them.*)

VICKI: Doctor, they're catching us up.

THE DOCTOR: Come along, come along.

(*They come to an intersection.* THE DOCTOR *points the way ahead.*)

There's the way out. Come along. We'll make it.

(*They reach the entrance,* THE DOCTOR *a little way ahead of* VICKI, *who turns to look behind her.*)

5. *Exterior Rill Centre.*

(THE DOCTOR *emerges and turns back to*
VICKI. *As she is about to exit, a heavy
iron grille slams down in front of her.
She grips the bars frantically and looks
out.*)

VICKI: Doctor!

(VICKI *turns as the* CHUMBLEY *sounds
grow louder.* THE DOCTOR *runs over and
examines the bars.*)

THE DOCTOR: Don't move, Vicki. I'll see if I can...

(*He grasps the grille and tries desper-
ately to push it up.*)

It won't move. There's no way of opening
it.

(THE DOCTOR *looks around and sees the
mechanism on the wall that he examined
before.*)

A-ha! Perhaps I'll be able to do a little
sabotage.

(*He moves across to the mechanism and
takes out a screwdriver from his pocket.*
VICKI *waits, grasping the bars whilst
looking behind her, expecting the* CHUM-
BLIES *at any minute.* THE DOCTOR *quickly
examines the air-converter unit.*)

Well I think we know what this is used for... converting air into ammonia.

VICKI: Hurry, Doctor!

THE DOCTOR: Yes, don't worry child, when I've finished with this, they'll soon release you.

(He continues to work on the mechanism.)

VICKI: What good will that do? Try and release these bars.

THE DOCTOR: Now that would be a waste of time. But this converter supplies the gas they breathe.

VICKI: But you don't know that!

THE DOCTOR: The Rills never come outside, Vicki. It seems a logical conclusion.

(VICKI turns once more and looks down the passageway.)

6. *INTERIOR PASSAGEWAY.*

(A CHUMBLEY moves along the passageway and reaches VICKI. THE DOCTOR appears on the other side of the bars and looks in. The CHUMBLEY makes signs just as the one they first met did.)

VICKI: It wants me to go with it.

THE DOCTOR: Then I'm afraid you'll have to do so.

VICKI: But that... that thing that was watching us in there...

THE DOCTOR: One of the Rills. Yes, must have been.

VICKI: Doctor, I'm frightened.

THE DOCTOR: Listen, my dear. If you go along quietly and cause no trouble, it will give me time to see if I can help you. I think I can do something with this air-converter, but I must have time.

VICKI: Yes, all right.

(VICKI eyes the CHUMBLEY and moves towards it. The CHUMBLEY backs away.)

7. INTERIOR PASSAGEWAY.

(VICKI moves down a passageway followed by the CHUMBLEY. Another CHUMBLEY moves to meet her and they nudge her towards the central chamber.)

8. EXTERIOR RILL CENTRE.

(THE DOCTOR moves away from the bars and resumes work on the air-converter with his screwdriver.)

9. INTERIOR DRAHVIN SPACESHIP.

(STEVEN is still in the padded corner. He is lying down, apparently asleep.)

DRAHVIN TWO: Maaga, shall we go?

MAAGA: Where?

DRAHVIN TWO: To patrol.

MAAGA: I see no need.

DRAHVIN TWO: To see what the other two are doing.

MAAGA: No.

DRAHVIN TWO: But, Maaga...

MAAGA: Can't you hear what I say!

DRAHVIN TWO: We always go out on patrol at this time.

MAAGA: Well, not now.

(The three DRAHVINS look uneasily at each other.)

Soldier Drahvins. You can't understand anything that's different, can you? You're made unintelligent, and you remain that way all your lives.

(MAAGA turns away, talking almost to herself.)

I told them soldiers were useless for space work. All they can do is kill. But no one listened. To conquer space, they said, you will need soldiers. And now here I am, confronted with danger, and the only one able to think.

(She turns back to the others.)

Very well. I am your commanding officer, am I not? I am your controller.

DRAHVIN TWO: Yes, Maaga.

MAAGA: And my orders are obeyed?

DRAHVIN TWO: Yes, Maaga.

MAAGA: Why?

DRAHVIN TWO: Because you are our leader.

MAAGA: And?

DRAHVIN TWO: You think.

MAAGA: And you don't know what that means?

(The DRAHVINS *are silent.)*

I order that there will be no patrol now we have a prisoner. In order to save him, the other two must help us.

DRAHVIN ONE: I do not understand why they would want to rescue a friend.

MAAGA: I don't suppose you do.

DRAHVIN ONE: We would not. We would leave him.

MAAGA: Yes, we would. But I have heard of beings

	like these. They help each other.
DRAHVIN THREE:	Why, Maaga?
MAAGA:	I don't know. But sometimes, I am told, they even die for each other.
DRAHVIN THREE:	Die? For their friends?
MAAGA:	Yes, there are many strange things in the Universe.
DRAHVIN TWO:	I do not understand.
MAAGA:	I know you don't understand. But, despite that, you will obey orders.

(The three DRAHVINS *bow their heads submissively. After a pause,* MAAGA *speaks quietly, almost to herself.)*

Maybe we will not kill either the Rills or these Earth creatures. Not with our own hands, that is. Perhaps it would be better to escape in the spaceship, and leave them here. Then, when we are out in space, we can look back. We will see a vast, white, exploding planet... and we will know that they have died with it.

DRAHVIN ONE: But we will not see them die.

MAAGA: You will not. But I, at least, have enough intelligence to imagine it. The fear. The terror. The shuddering of a planet at the end of its life. And they die. But that is for later...

(She turns back to the DRAHVINS *and issues instructions to them each, in turn.)*

Attention! You will sleep... you will stand watch for the Earth men... and you will remain on guard. To your stations. Open the door.

*(*DRAHVIN ONE *moves round the table, picking up her gun as she does so. She crosses to a chair near* STEVEN *and sits down , the gun across her lap. The other* DRAHVINS *go into the inner room.* MAAGA *goes over and looks down at* STEVEN.*)*

DRAHVIN ONE: He sleeps.

MAAGA: But you will not. He is not to move.

*(*DRAHVIN ONE *nods in obeyance.* MAAGA *goes into the inner room. As she does so,* STEVEN *opens his eyes slightly and squints up at* DRAHVIN ONE, *who is staring straight ahead.)*

10. INTERIOR RILL CENTRAL CHAMBER.

(A CHUMBLEY *backs in followed by*

VICKI. *She searches about her and looks nervously at the place where she saw the watching eyes. The shutter on the door is closed. Another* CHUMBLEY *comes out of the passageway. The two* CHUMBLIES *chatter to themselves for a moment, then, from the* CHUMBLEY *facing* VICKI, *comes a high-pitched sound.* VICKI *stares at it blankly. It stops, twitters at her once or twice more, then falls silent. The* CHUMBLEY *behind* VICKI *nudges her. She puts up with this for a few moments, then angrily reacts.)*

VICKI: Don't do that! What do you want, anyway?

(At once a series of varying sounds comes from the CHUMBLEY, *then suddenly...)*

CHUMBLEY: Don't do that, what do you want anyway? Don't do that, what do you want anyway?

(There is a chattering sound, then silence. Then from the CHUMBLEY, *as though it has now deciphered* VICKI'S *words, comes intelligible speech.)*

We are sorry to separate you from your friends, but it was necessary.

*(*VICKI *is surprised. She jumps as the shutter barring the* RILLS *from her slides*

open. A RILL *can be seen looking through at her.* VICKI *looks from the* RILL *to the* CHUMBLEY.*)*

VICKI: Who are you?

CHUMBLEY: Who are you?

VICKI: We're... we're time travellers. From the planet Earth.

(There is a pause as the RILL *studies her.)*

CHUMBLEY: I see. You were sent here by the Drahvins?

VICKI: Yes.

CHUMBLEY: To do us harm.

VICKI: No, no. The Drahvins are holding a friend of ours prisoner. We had to do as they told us.

CHUMBLEY: What was that?

*(*VICKI *reluctantly replies.)*

VICKI: To help them capture your ship.

CHUMBLEY: Why do they want to capture it? We have offered to take them with us.

VICKI: They didn't tell us that.

*(*VICKI *moves slightly as she speaks. The other* CHUMBLEY *hustles her back into place.)*

CHUMBLEY: No. They would not. They would rather kill. They hate us.

VICKI: Well, you did try to kill one of them.

CHUMBLEY: We kill no-one.

(VICKI, who is still being pushed by the other CHUMBLEY, is suddenly exasperated.)

VICKI: Look, who is talking? Is it... this Chumbley, or is it...

(She looks towards the open shutters.)

... someone else?

CHUMBLEY: You call the machines Chumblies?

VICKI: Yes.

CHUMBLEY: The Chumblies have a speaker in them. They are transmitting our thoughts.

VICKI: Your... thoughts?

CHUMBLEY: We do not speak like you. We have no vocal chords. We communicate in thought.

VICKI: But who are you?

CHUMBLEY: We are the Rills.

VICKI: Then why can't I see you?

CHUMBLEY: It is better that you do not. Not all the dominant species in the Universe look like men. Our appearance might shock you as it shocked the Drahvins.

11. *Exterior Rill Centre.*

(THE DOCTOR *has now removed some of the top plates from the air converter and is peering in. He is hard at work with his screwdriver.*)

12. *Interior Rill Central Chamber.*

VICKI: The Drahvins said you attacked them.

CHUMBLEY: That is short of the truth. We were investigating outer space when we encountered a strange ship. Rills do not attack or kill without good reason, so we stopped our ship. Their ship also stopped. We hung in space facing each other. We would have turned and gone away, but we were afraid that we would be attacked.

VICKI: What happened?

CHUMBLEY: For four dawns we hung there. Then we decided to turn. As we were doing so the Drahvins fired. Immediately we did the same, and both ships crashed. When we escaped from our ship we discovered that we could not breathe the atmosphere here, but we had a small supply of our own, and set out to help the Drahvins....

(As the RILL *speaks through the* CHUMB-LEY, *we see what happened as a flash-back through the* RILL's *eyes.)*

13. EXTERIOR (DAY).

(Glimpses of other RILLS *can be seen, but none clearly, as they are at the edge of vision. As the* RILL *looks around, a* DRAHVIN *is seen, lying face down on the ground.)*

CHUMBLEY *(oov)*: The first one we found was badly injured. We started to help the soldier.
Then Maaga, their leader appeared. She threatened to shoot us, so we left.

*(*MAAGA *fires.)*

14. INTERIOR RILL CENTRAL CHAMBER (EVENING).

VICKI: Why didn't you shoot back?

CHUMBLEY: We could have done. Our weapons are superior to theirs. But we do not kill. The Drahvins do.

15. EXTERIOR (DAY).

*(*MAAGA *aims her gun at the injured* DRAHVIN *and fires.)*

CHUMBLEY
(oov):

When we looked back, we saw Maaga kill the injured soldier.

> 16. *Interior Rill Central Chamber (Evening).*

VICKI:

But all the Drahvins believe that you did it.

CHUMBLEY:

We know. That is why they keep attacking us.

VICKI:

Would you really have taken them off with you, in your ship?

CHUMBLEY:

Why not? What do we gain if they die?

(VICKI *looks at the* RILL *through the open shutters.)*

We will help you rescue your friend.

(VICKI *does not respond.)*

Something is worrying you?

VICKI:

I... I wish I could see the whole you.

CHUMBLEY:

It is better that you don't. Besides, we cannot come out. In order to live we must have ammoniac gas. So we live in a compartment where it is filtered in...

(VICKI *reacts in horror.)*

VICKI:

You can't breathe oxygen at all?

CHUMBLEY: No. Our home planet is...

(VICKI *tries to leave but the* CHUMBLEY *blocks her path.*)

What is it?

VICKI: Let me out. Quickly. Please! Or you'll all be killed!

CHUMBLEY: Killed? By whom?

VICKI: The Doctor. He's wrecking your machine for making ammoniac gas.

17. EXTERIOR RILL CENTRE.

(THE DOCTOR *is working feverishly at the air-converter mechanism with his screwdriver, talking to himself.*)

THE DOCTOR: Now come along Doctor, come along. There's not much time, you know...

(*He continues to disassemble the converter.*)

18. INTERIOR DRAHVIN SPACESHIP.

(STEVEN *is still pretending to be asleep, but is squinting at the* DRAHVIN *that is guarding him, who is herself nodding off to sleep. Slowly,* STEVEN *eases himself up into a sitting position. He eases his legs down to the floor. There is a creak.*

The DRAHVIN *reacts slightly, but continues to doze.* STEVEN *slowly reaches
towards the* DRAHVIN's *gun. Then with
one movement he snatches the gun,
clasps a hand over the* DRAHVIN's *mouth
and keeps moving forward, so that the*
DRAHVIN *and the chair she is sitting on
topple over backwards. Holding the gun,*
STEVEN *prepares to cover the* DRAHVIN,
*but he realises that the fall has knocked
her unconscious. He listens. All is silent.
He moves towards the lever that opens
the door. There is a humming sound and
the door begins to slide open. At the
same time, the door to* MAAGA's *compartment opens, and* MAAGA *stands
there, gun in hand.)*

MAAGA: He is escaping!

*(*STEVEN *leaps towards the outer door,
but it is closed. He turns back to see*
MAAGA, *by now joined by the other*
DRAHVINS, *approaching. He points his
gun at them.)*

STEVEN: Stop!

(They halt. MAAGA *comes forward.)*

MAAGA: You cannot escape. Give up and we will
not harm you.

STEVEN: I'd be a fool to believe that, wouldn't I?

(He glances to the side and sees two buttons on the wall. Still pointing his gun at the DRAHVINS *he presses one button and the inner door slides shut, sealing him off from the* DRAHVINS. *He presses the other button and the outer door opens. He exits.)*

19. *EXTERIOR DRAHVIN SPACESHIP.*

*(*STEVEN *emerges and looks warily about. He is about to move off when he sees a* CHUMBLEY *approaching. He stares at it, gun at the ready, then looks back at the spaceship. He makes his decision and heads back into the airlock. He presses the button to close the outer door, and as it closes behind him, the* CHUMBLEY *moves in and waits. He turns towards the inner door and, through the porthole in the door, is startled to see* MAAGA *standing there, a cruel smirking grin on her face.)*

20. *EXTERIOR RILL CENTRE.*

*(*THE DOCTOR *is reaching into the machine. With a grunt of pleasure he brings out a small metal plate and drops it on the ground. Then he peers in again.)*

THE DOCTOR: Now then, all we have to do is...

              (He picks up the screwdriver and poises it over the machine.)

VICKI *(oov)*:   Doctor... No!

              (THE DOCTOR turns in surprise.)

              Don't do it, please!

              (THE DOCTOR moves away from the machine and VICKI and the CHUMBLEY come into view from the passageway, as the bars slide up out of sight.)

              I was afraid I'd be too late.

THE DOCTOR: My dear child, are you all right?

VICKI: Yes, yes, the Rills won't harm us. They want to help.

CHUMBLEY: We were told your friend is in danger.

              (THE DOCTOR starts back, suprised by the fact that the CHUMBLEY can talk.)

THE DOCTOR: I take it that is a Rill talking.

VICKI: Yes. Well go on, answer him.

THE DOCTOR: You were told correctly.

CHUMBLEY: Then perhaps you will both come inside.

THE DOCTOR: It occurs to me that if we do that we could both be trapped.

VICKI: Doctor, if they meant us any harm, this Chumbley could shoot us now...

THE DOCTOR: Yes, yes, quite true he could. Very well, lead the way. I'd like to have a good look round as it happens.

(The CHUMBLEY *turns and leads the way back. As they move another* CHUMBLEY *passes them, going in the opposite direction.)*

THE DOCTOR: Hello, where's he going?

CHUMBLEY: To repair the damage you have done.

THE DOCTOR: Ah.

(He nods to himself, looks apologetic and grimaces at VICKI. *They move down the passageway. Meanwhile, the other* CHUMBLEY *reaches the air converter and starts to examine it, making the usual chumbley sounds as it does.)*

21. INTERIOR PASSAGEWAY.

*(*THE DOCTOR *and* VICKI *move along after the* CHUMBLEY.*)*

THE DOCTOR: What were the Rills like, my child?

VICKI: They won't show themselves, Doctor.

THE DOCTOR: Why ever not?

(The CHUMBLEY *halts and turns.)*

CHUMBLEY: Because our appearance would not be pleasant to you.

THE DOCTOR: Nonsense! Do you think we're children?

CHUMBLEY: It is best that you do not see us.

(The CHUMBLEY *turns and moves off.)*

THE DOCTOR: Oh, very well. Please yourselves. Such foolishness...

(They move off after the CHUMBLEY.*)*

22. *INTERIOR RILL CENTRAL CHAMBER.*

(The CHUMBLEY *enters and halts, followed by* THE DOCTOR *and* VICKI. THE DOCTOR *looks round and taps the* CHUMBLEY *with his stick.)*

THE DOCTOR: What are you drilling for, may I ask?

CHUMBLEY: Power. We must have power for launching our spaceship. The suns are too weak to supply this power, therefore by drilling we may find some in the ground.

THE DOCTOR: Then if you'll take my advice you'll find it quickly. You don't have much time.

CHUMBLEY: You know about the explosion of this planet?

THE DOCTOR:	We know more than you. Your timing is wrong. The disintegration is now less than two dawns.
CHUMBLEY:	Two dawns. Then we have no chance of survival.
VICKI:	But you finished repairing the ship?
CHUMBLEY:	Yes. But the only power we find is a gas, and that is of no use to us. We have no means of converting it into the sun-ray power we need.
THE DOCTOR:	I must be able to supply the power you need as you are going to help us.
CHUMBLEY:	We would be deeply grateful.
VICKI:	And that's another thing. You keep saying we. How many of you are there?
CHUMBLEY:	Four.
VICKI:	That doesn't seem many for manning a spaceship.
CHUMBLEY:	We were twelve. Eight of us died in the crash.

(THE DOCTOR *nods sympathetically, then is immediately business-like.*)

THE DOCTOR:	I shall require some metal-cored cable.
CHUMBLEY:	We have some.
THE DOCTOR:	Good. I think we might be able to effect a

transference of power from our ship to this. But you'll have to do a little conversion first. Can you do that?

CHUMBLEY: We shall do all that you say, you are our only...

(The CHUMBLEY *stops talking and starts chittering. There is the sound of machinery, as though from a control panel in the* RILLS' *chamber.)*

THE DOCTOR: What's the matter? What's happening?

CHUMBLEY: We have just received a message from a machine.

VICKI: A Chumbley?

CHUMBLEY: It is by the Drahvin spaceship. It reports that a being, not Drahvin, came out of it...

VICKI: Steven!

CHUMBLEY: It detected that he was a friend of yours, but before contact could be made he went back in again.

VICKI: He still thinks you are dangerous.

CHUMBLEY: Let me go and tell him.

THE DOCTOR: Mmm. Well, at least he can take care of himself. Now let's get this cable out.

23. INTERIOR DRAHVIN AIRLOCK.

(STEVEN *is looking out at the* CHUMBLEY.
He looks up when MAAGA's *voice comes
from a loudspeaker in the airlock.*)

MAAGA *(oov)*: Do you hear me, Earthman?

STEVEN: I hear you.

MAAGA: If you throw your gun down, we will open
the airlock.

(STEVEN *looks at his gun and grips it
tighter.*)

Very well, but if you try to come through
here you may kill one or two of my soldiers. But we will kill you.

(STEVEN *turns and looks through the
outer door.*)

Yes, outside the Rills' machine waits for
you. To kill also.

STEVEN: Then I'll stay here. I may be trapped, but
you can't harm me.

MAAGA: You are in the airlock. On the wall are
some dials... they are pressure gauges.

(STEVEN *looks towards them.*)

STEVEN: So?

MAAGA: We can draw the oxygen out of that section. You will suffocate.

(STEVEN *looks around and moves to touch the button that opens the outer door.*)

If you touch that, the door will open completely, leaving you at the mercy of the machine.

24. *INTERIOR DRAHVIN SPACESHIP.*

(MAAGA *signals to the* DRAHVINS. DRAHVIN TWO *and* DRAHVIN THREE *move to the wall and grasp a wheel.*)

DRAHVIN TWO: Ready.

MAAGA: Pressure?

DRAHVIN TWO: Normal.

MAAGA: Temperature?

DRAHVIN TWO: Normal.

MAAGA: Good. Empty airlock.

(*The* DRAHVINS *start to turn the wheel.*)

25. *INTERIOR DRAHVIN AIRLOCK.*

(STEVEN *looks at one of the dials. The needle is flickering and drops very slightly.*)

MAAGA: Yes, Earthman. The air is leaving the airlock. You have three choices.

STEVEN: Three?

MAAGA: Die in there. Come back and die here, or go out and be killed by the machine.

             (STEVEN *looks around desperately. The needle on the dial drops further.*)

             26. INTERIOR RILL CENTRAL CHAMBER.

             (VICKI *is helping* THE DOCTOR *with some cable. The* CHUMBLIES *are there and the* RILL *watches from the other side of the shuttered door.*)

THE DOCTOR: Good. Good. That should be enough to do it. Let me have your arm, I'll lay the cable to my ship... follow me.

CHUMBLEY: Our thanks.

             (*There are more noises from the control panel.*)

VICKI: What's that?

CHUMBLEY: The Chumbley has reported that your friend is still in the ship. But he is making noises that it cannot understand. It says they sound like cries of distress.

VICKI: Doctor!

THE DOCTOR: We must go at once.

CHUMBLEY: You cannot help him alone. We will send

two more Chumbley machines with you.

THE DOCTOR: What can they do?

CHUMBLEY: Cut open the ship, if necessary.

> (*Another* CHUMBLEY *enters the room, its light flashing furiously.*)

Go. Quickly. The Chumbley reports that the sounds are weakening.

VICKI: Come on, Doctor!

THE DOCTOR: Vicki, stay here!

VICKI: No, I'm coming with you.

> (THE DOCTOR *is annoyed but has no time to argue. He turns to the* CHUMBLEY *who has been speaking.*)

THE DOCTOR: Oh, come on then... and you stay here until you receive a message.

CHUMBLEY: Yes, I will do that.

> (THE DOCTOR *and* VICKI *follow the other* CHUMBLIES *into the passageway.*)

27. INTERIOR RILL PASSAGEWAY.

(*The* CHUMBLIES, THE DOCTOR *and* VICKI *rush along the corridor.*)

28. EXTERIOR RILL CENTRE.

(The CHUMBLIES *exit, followed by* THE DOCTOR *and* VICKI. *Together, they hurry off in the direction of the* DRAHVIN *spaceship.)*

29. EXTERIOR DRAHVIN SPACESHIP.

(They approach the DRAHVINS' *spaceship. Without warning,* DRAHVIN ONE *appears. She aims her gun at them.)*

DRAHVIN ONE: Halt or I fire.

THE DOCTOR: What is wrong?

DRAHVIN ONE: Where are you going?

THE DOCTOR: Back to your spaceship of course.

DRAHVIN ONE: The machines are our enemies. Why do you bring them with you?

THE DOCTOR: They are going to help you and Maaga and the rest get to the Rills' spaceship. We wish to save lives, not destroy them.

DRAHVIN ONE: Maaga doesn't trust you. I do not trust you.

VICKI: We've captured these two machines. They do as we tell them. Watch... Go forward... Stop... Come back.

(The CHUMBLIES *do as* VICKI *commands.)*

You see?

(DRAHVIN ONE *turns and fires at one of the* CHUMBLIES. VICKI *struggles with her and manages to get the gun.*)

THE DOCTOR: Take care, Vicki.

DRAHVIN ONE: Kill me now, I have failed in my duty.

THE DOCTOR: Nonsense. Stop this thought of killing anyone. Come back to your ship.

VICKI: Go on, and hurry up.

(*The* CHUMBLIES *chitter away, sending a message back to the* RILL *centre.*)

30. *INTERIOR DRAHVIN AIRLOCK.*

(STEVEN *is now much the worse for wear. His mouth is wide open and he is gasping for air.*)

MAAGA: Why do you not give up, Earthman?

STEVEN: I'd rather face the Chumblies than you, any day.

(*He stares in hatred at* MAAGA *through the porthole, fighting for breath. He almost drops his gun, but manages to retain it. He staggers against the wall and rests his forehead and palms against it. He tries to push the outer door button.*)

MAAGA: That will not work now the pressure has locked the doors. Soon you will be dead.

(The dial is now very low. It drops further. STEVEN *starts to slide down against the wall.)*

Next Episode:
THE EXPLODING PLANET

EPISODE FOUR

THE EXPLODING PLANET

1. *Interior Drahvin Airlock.*

(STEVEN *is now much the worse for wear. His mouth is wide open and he is gasping for air.*)

MAAGA: Why do you not give up, Earthman?

STEVEN: I'd rather face the Chumblies than you, any day.

(*He stares in hatred at* MAAGA *through the porthole, fighting for breath. He almost drops his gun, but manages to retain it. He staggers against the wall and rests his forehead and palms against it. He tries to push the outer door button.*)

MAAGA: That will not work now the pressure has locked the doors. Soon you will be dead.

(*The dial is now very low. It drops further.* STEVEN *starts to slide down against the wall.*)

2. *Exterior Drahvin Spaceship.*

(One of the CHUMBLIES *moves towards the spaceship.)*

3. *Interior Drahvin Spaceship.*

DRAHVIN TWO: Soon he will die.

MAAGA: We do not want him dead.

DRAHVIN TWO: But Maaga, he is our enemy.

MAAGA: But also our hostage.

DRAHVIN THREE: Machine approaching... with bomb.

MAAGA: Quick, take cover!

(As she speaks, a projectile crashes through the porthole and lands on the floor, and immediately begins to discharge a thick cloud of ammonia.)

4. *Exterior Drahvin Spaceship.*

*(*STEVEN *appears at the window, near collapse. A* CHUMBLEY *fires its gun at the door. The door flies open, there is a hissing of air and* STEVEN *tumbles out. He draws back at the sight of the* CHUMBLEY.*)*

CHUMBLEY: All right, it's quite safe now.

(VICKI *rushes over to* STEVEN.)

VICKI: Oh Steven, are you okay?

STEVEN: Yes, thanks. You got here just in time.

(THE DOCTOR *hurries over.*)

THE DOCTOR: You're sure you're all right?

STEVEN: I will be in a moment. Thanks for helping.

THE DOCTOR: Hmm, it was the Chumblies, actually. Our friends, the Drahvins, won't be pleased.

5. *INTERIOR DRAHVIN SPACESHIP.*

(*The* DRAHVINS *are standing before* MAAGA, *who is furious.*)

MAAGA: Guns ready.

(*The* DRAHVINS *bring up their guns.*)

Door.

(DRAHVIN TWO *runs over and presses the button.*)

After them and kill.

(*They head for the door.*)

6. *EXTERIOR DRAHVIN SPACESHIP.*

(*The* DRAHVINS *surge out of the airlock.*)

CHUMBLEY: Stop!

(The DRAHVINS *come to a halt as they see the* CHUMBLEY's *ray-gun pointing at them.)*

If you move we shall fire. Do not mistake our intention. It is to kill if you interfere.

(The DRAHVINS *remain still. One of the* CHUMBLIES *bumps into* THE DOCTOR.*)*

Doctor, please bring your party away.

THE DOCTOR: Certainly. Can you walk, young man?

STEVEN: I think so.

THE DOCTOR: Come along then...

*(*STEVEN *stands, swaying a little.* VICKI *supports him.)*

CHUMBLEY: Come.

(The CHUMBLEY *turns and the three travellers follow. One of the other* CHUMBLIES *stands guard over the three* DRAHVINS. MAAGA *appears at the doorway, careful not to show herself to the* CHUMBLEY.*)*

You will take your soldiers back into the ship and you will stay there.

*(*MAAGA *glares out at the scene before her.)*

Until now we have spared you, although you have attacked us time and time again. But we will always defend our friends.

(MAAGA *mutters scornfully under her breath.*)

MAAGA: Friends!

CHUMBLEY: We will prevent any attempt on your part to leave the ship. I am resolute, now go back into your spaceship.

MAAGA: The air is made foul by your bomb.

CHUMBLEY: It will have cleared by now. The ammonia bomb was only a warning. Go inside.

(MAAGA *turns, realising that for now, she is powerless.*)

MAAGA: Come.

(*The* DRAHVINS *re-enter their spaceship. The* CHUMBLEY *stands watch outside.*)

7. *INTERIOR DRAHVIN SPACESHIP.*

(MAAGA *crosses to a porthole and looks out as the three* DRAHVINS *enter.*)

MAAGA: It is still there.

DRAHVIN TWO: We can't escape.

MAAGA: Quiet.

DRAHVIN ONE: But Maaga, we...

MAAGA: We cannot escape yet. But we will. No Drahvin is defeated until dead. Is that correct?

(The three DRAHVINS *reply in unison.)*

DRAHVINS: Yes, Maaga.

MAAGA: And we are still alive. It is a question of how long that machine will be. You failed in your mission of patrol.

DRAHVIN ONE: I was outnumbered.

MAAGA: You will be dealt with, failure is not tolerated. Three. Does the forward hatch still operate?

DRAHVIN THREE: Yes, Maaga.

MAAGA: Silently?

DRAHVIN THREE: Yes, Maaga.

MAAGA: It is now dim light. Then it will finally be night. The last night this planet will know. We must capture the Rill ship before then. When I give the signal, you will leave silently through the forward hatch. You will then circle round behind the machine. Understood?

DRAHVIN THREE:	Yes, Maaga.
MAAGA:	And you will destroy it.

8. *INTERIOR RILL CENTRAL CHAMBER.*

(THE DOCTOR, STEVEN *and* VICKI *enter.* THE DOCTOR *immediately moves across to where the cable is, with a* CHUMBLEY.)

STEVEN: Smells strange.

VICKI: That's the ammoniac gas we told you about.

STEVEN: I'd rather they breathed it than me.

(VICKI *leaves* STEVEN *and moves across to* THE DOCTOR.)

VICKI: Doctor, there can't be much time left.

THE DOCTOR: About six hours, I should think.

(*He turns to the* CHUMBLEY.)

Did you finish the conversion?

CHUMBLEY: Yes, we did. But it will take hours to transfer the power of your ship to ours.

THE DOCTOR: Oh, rubbish, rubbish.

CHUMBLEY: We are concerned for your safety.

VICKI: And we're concerned for yours.

THE DOCTOR:	Yes, yes, very noble of you indeed, but this is a matter of emergency, now bring the cable.
CHUMBLEY:	Very well.
STEVEN:	What's going on?
THE DOCTOR:	I'm going to transfer some power from my ship to the Rills.
STEVEN:	Oh, I see. Do you want me to stay here?
THE DOCTOR:	Yes, you stay here with the leader of the Rills. Should you suspect anything wrong, contact me immediately. You stay here, there's no danger now.
VICKI:	Can I come with you, Doctor?
THE DOCTOR:	If you wish.

(THE DOCTOR and VICKI leave. STEVEN walks around the chamber.)

CHUMBLEY:	You have not gone with your friends.
STEVEN:	No.
CHUMBLEY:	You are interested in our place?
STEVEN:	Quite. So the Doctor trusts you?
CHUMBLEY:	Why shouldn't he?
STEVEN:	No reason. I'm sure you produced the right ethical reasons for him and so naturally he does.

CHUMBLEY: We rescued you from the Drahvins, but you still don't trust us?

STEVEN: You may be like them, using us for your own salvation.

CHUMBLEY: The Doctor offered to help us. We needed his help.

STEVEN: So did the Drahvins.

CHUMBLEY: What are you getting at?

STEVEN: Nothing.

CHUMBLEY: Yes you are.

STEVEN: All right. You said it would take hours to charge your ship.

CHUMBLEY: The Doctor said he could do it in time.

STEVEN: Suppose, just this once, you were right and he was wrong. Would you take us with you or would you allow us to leave in our own ship?

CHUMBLEY: In your own ship... if possible.

STEVEN: Come off it. If there wasn't time to finish charging your ship, you wouldn't let us go just like that.

CHUMBLEY: We are strange beings to you. You've never met anything like us. You come from Earth, a planet we don't know, but clearly it is a planet which still knows conflict.

STEVEN: So?

CHUMBLEY: If we are right and the power-charge is going to take too long a time, then the Doctor, the girl and you must leave. We believe in self-preservation.

STEVEN: I'm sure you do.

CHUMBLEY: But if there is a choice, the Doctor must go. He travels further than we can. And everything he has shown he stands for is what we believe in; so it is better that he goes.

STEVEN: You can't blame me for being suspicious. There's something you should know. While I was in the Drahvin spaceship they said they were determined to leave in your ship.

CHUMBLEY: We are prepared to take them with us.

STEVEN: That's not what they mean. They take your ship, you stay here.

CHUMBLEY: We must hope they don't succeed.

STEVEN: With time running out they'll be desperate, so let me help you fix the cable at this end.

CHUMBLEY: Thank you. The machine will help you. It will be quicker.

STEVEN: It's got to be.

9. *INTERIOR DRAHVIN SPACESHIP.*

(DRAHVIN THREE *is opening the hatch.* MAAGA *stands nearby.*)

DRAHVIN THREE:

Ready, Maaga.

MAAGA:

Then go.

(*She puts an iron bar about three feet long by four inches thick into* DRAHVIN THREE's *hands.*)

And do not fail!

DRAHVIN THREE:

I shall not.

(*She exits through the hatch.*)

10. *EXTERIOR DRAHVIN SPACESHIP.*

(DRAHVIN THREE *emerges and drops silently to the ground. She pauses, grasps the bar firmly and looks about, then moves off. The hatch door is closed again from within. At the other side of the ship, the* CHUMBLEY *stands guard, unaware of what has just occurred.*)

11. *EXTERIOR THE TARDIS.*

(THE DOCTOR *and* VICKI *approach the*

TARDIS, followed by the CHUMBLEY, *the cable snaking out behind him.* THE DOCTOR *moves to the door of the police box and searches for his key.* VICKI *looks around.)*

VICKI:　　　　It's getting darker now, Doctor.

THE DOCTOR:　Yes, nothing to worry about. Evening here must last about four hours.

　　　　　　　(THE DOCTOR *finds his key and opens the door.)*

VICKI:　　　　Isn't it strange to think that all of this will explode into nothing at dawn?

THE DOCTOR:　Not nothing... Hydrogen gas, splaying itself out like molten stars in the same galaxy.

12. INTERIOR DRAHVIN SPACESHIP.

*(*DRAHVIN ONE *and* DRAHVIN TWO *are seated at the table.* MAAGA *stares out through a porthole.)*

MAAGA:　　　　I cannot see her.

DRAHVIN ONE:　She will die willingly.

MAAGA:　　　　She will not die until she eliminates that machine.

DRAHVIN TWO:　Will we escape, Maaga?

MAAGA: Once we have wrecked that machine, yes. We will escape.

(As she speaks, the ship rocks violently.)

DRAHVIN TWO: What is happening?

MAAGA: It's first warning of the explosion. We have only five hours. She must work quickly.

13. EXTERIOR DRAHVIN SPACESHIP.

*(*DRAHVIN THREE *creeps towards the* CHUMBLEY. *She comes up behind it and, raising the bar high over her head, brings it crashing down with murderous force.)*

14. EXTERIOR THE TARDIS (NIGHT).

(The cable leads from the door of the TARDIS out across the landscape.)

15. INTERIOR RILL CENTRAL CHAMBER.

(The cable runs from the passageway into the chamber.)

THE DOCTOR: Everything under control. Start motors.

CHUMBLEY: Start control. Full intake. Cable guard stand by.

VICKI:	Is the power being transferred?
THE DOCTOR:	Hmm? Oh, yes, yes it is.
VICKI:	How long will it take?
THE DOCTOR:	Three or four hours I should think, the exact time's being worked out now.
STEVEN:	But the planet's going to explode in less than five hours.
THE DOCTOR:	Yes, I quite appreciate that fact, young man.

(THE DOCTOR *is cut short by a loud noise from the control panel.*)

VICKI:	There's that alarm again.
STEVEN:	What's happened now?

(A CHUMBLEY *moves towards them.* THE DOCTOR *turns round.*)

CHUMBLEY:	Silence, please. Emergency message coming through... The Drahvins have escaped and destroyed the Chumbley outside their spaceship.
VICKI:	Oh, no!
THE DOCTOR:	What of the Chumbley outside my TARDIS?
CHUMBLEY:	In the position he has taken up he is in no danger. Continue, Doctor... there will be

no more incidents.

STEVEN: I don't think they'll go after the TARDIS anyway. It's this ship they want... and us.

16. EXTERIOR DRAHVIN SPACESHIP.

*(*MAAGA, DRAHVIN ONE *and* DRAHVIN TWO *climb through the hatch.* MAAGA *looks round, peering into the night.* DRAHVIN THREE *moves to join her.)*

MAAGA: You have done well.

DRAHVIN
THREE: Thank you, Maaga.

MAAGA: I shall see that you are mentioned. Did you see any other machines?

DRAHVIN
THREE: The only one that was there I destroyed.

MAAGA: Good.

DRAHVIN
THREE: It will not move again.

*(*DRAHVIN ONE *and* DRAHVIN TWO *nod in pleasurable understanding.)*

MAAGA: We are going to attack the Rill centre. You will keep close behind me. Understand?

(The three DRAHVINS *all nod.)*

When we are nearer, I will give you further orders. Come.

(They move off across the planet, holding their guns at the ready.)

17. *INTERIOR RILL CENTRAL CHAMBER.*

(THE DOCTOR is trying to calm STEVEN, who is very agitated.)

THE DOCTOR: Do stop worrying, dear boy.

CHUMBLEY: Stand still.

(THE DOCTOR, STEVEN and VICKI stand still, as the CHUMBLIES stream this way and that.)

STEVEN: Now look. I know what they intend to do. As soon as they see that cable they will destroy it.

CHUMBLEY: Do not worry. I am prepared for that.

THE DOCTOR: I'm sure they are. Is the power still coming through?

CHUMBLEY: It is.

STEVEN: How long is it going to be?

CHUMBLEY: Another two hours, at least.

THE DOCTOR: Well, that should be enough.

VICKI: Just.

STEVEN: Isn't it possible to charge faster?

THE DOCTOR: Utterly impossible. The control panel would be blown out.

STEVEN: How are we going to get back to the TARDIS in time?

THE DOCTOR: Hmm?

STEVEN: The Drahvins are still determined to get us.

CHUMBLEY: Do not worry. We will ensure that you return safely to your ship.

(VICKI *tilts her head, as she hears the sound of gun-fire outside. She moves towards the exit.*)

VICKI: The Drahvins are out there!

STEVEN: They don't waste much time, do they?

(*The hissing of guns grows louder, then drops a little. Suddenly* DRAHVIN THREE *enters the chamber and points her gun at* STEVEN *and* VICKI, *who are standing apart from* THE DOCTOR, *who is by the door to the* RILLS' *chamber.*)

DRAHVIN THREE: Stand still!

(VICKI *and* STEVEN *stand frozen with fear.* THE DOCTOR *goes to move towards them, but before he can move, the* RILLS' *door opens and the* CHUMBLEY *pushes him though.* DRAHVIN THREE *still has* VICKI *and* STEVEN *in her sight.)*

DRAHVIN THREE: You escaped once, you will not do so again.

VICKI: She's going to kill us.

STEVEN: Then be killed herself.

DRAHVIN THREE: Death does not frighten me. I die as a warrior Drahvin.

(She starts to pull the trigger.)

Prepare to die.

(A CHUMBLEY *chitters in from one of the passageways and as it does so, it fires.* DRAHVIN THREE *stiffens, as though paralysed for a moment, then crumples to the floor.)*

STEVEN: What have you done?

CHUMBLEY: Do not worry, she is completely paralysed. I told you there would be no further incidents.

*(*VICKI *suddenly realises that* THE DOCTOR *is not with them.)*

VICKI: Doctor?

*(*THE DOCTOR'*s voice comes from within the* RILLS' *chamber.)*

THE DOCTOR (*oov*):	I'm in here. Come in... slowly.
CHUMBLEY:	You may enter. But be prepared for a shock.

(VICKI *looks at* STEVEN.)

VICKI:	Do you think we ought to?
THE DOCTOR (*oov*):	Come along. Come along.
STEVEN:	All right.

(STEVEN *and* VICKI *move towards the door, followed by the* CHUMBLEY.)

18. EXTERIOR.

(MAAGA, DRAHVIN ONE *and* DRAHVIN TWO *are on a ridge, resting.* MAAGA *looks around.* DRAHVIN TWO *is keeping watch.*)

MAAGA:	We have beaten them off.
DRAHVIN ONE:	Yes, Maaga... but we have not destroyed any.
MAAGA:	Don't worry, we will...

(DRAHVIN TWO *suddenly points.*)

DRAHVIN TWO:	More machines!
MAAGA:	Again!

(*Several* CHUMBLIES *move across the*

landscape.)

19. *INTERIOR RILL INNER CHAMBER.*

(Behind a glass partition are the RILLS. *They are enveloped in a dense, smoky gas.* THE DOCTOR *turns as* VICKI *and* STEVEN *enter the chamber.)*

CHUMBLEY: Now you know what we look like.

THE DOCTOR: Indeed we do. And I, at least, am glad of it.

CHUMBLEY: We apologise for the glass partition, but you will understand that we must keep our atmosphere in here.

THE DOCTOR: Of course, of course.

(The CHUMBLEY *moves towards him.)*

CHUMBLEY: Our appearance shocks you?

THE DOCTOR: No. Not now. It did at first.

STEVEN: I don't see why the Drahvins should hate you.

VICKI: I don't either. We probably look just as strange to you.

CHUMBLEY: To the Drahvins, we are ugly, so they become frightened.

THE DOCTOR: You are different from us, but you are intelligent life, as we are.

STEVEN: What does it matter what your form is?

THE DOCTOR: Importance lies in the character and what use is made of intelligence. We respect you as we respect all life.

(Without warning, VICKI *stumbles.* STEVEN *catches her.)*

STEVEN: Doctor!

THE DOCTOR: Hmm? What is it, child.

VICKI: Just that... just that I'm feeling terribly ill.

STEVEN: It's the ammoniac gas escaping.

THE DOCTOR: I should have thought of that.

CHUMBLEY: You had better return to the other chamber. Our atmosphere is not good for you.

THE DOCTOR: Indeed not. Take the child out, young man.

VICKI: I don't expect we shall see you again.

CHUMBLEY: It is improbable.

VICKI: Goodbye.

CHUMBLEY: Goodbye.

20. Interior Rill Central Chamber.

STEVEN: How much longer?

THE DOCTOR: One hour, I should think.

STEVEN: And how long before the explosion?

THE DOCTOR: About one and a half hours.

STEVEN: Well, I just hope that no more Drahvins get in.

21. *EXTERIOR PLANET LANDSCAPE.*

(MAAGA, DRAHVIN ONE *and* DRAHVIN TWO *take cover on top of the ridge. The* CHUMBLIES *fire on them and they fire back, but to no avail.* MAAGA *throws her gun to the ground in frustration and despair.*)

DRAHVIN ONE: Then we must attack them with bars, as Three did.

MAAGA: I cannot afford to lose any more soldiers.

(*She looks around, then points.*)

Get out that way. Head for the spaceship part of their building. We must concentrate on that. Come.

(*The* DRAHVINS *nod and set off.* MAAGA *retrieves her gun and in desperation fires again at the* CHUMBLIES.)

22. *INTERIOR RILL CENTRAL CHAMBER.*

STEVEN: How much longer?

THE DOCTOR: Patience, my dear fellow, patience.

VICKI: Dawn is only half an hour away.

STEVEN: And when dawn comes this planet explodes like a bomb.

THE DOCTOR: My goodness, you people.

(Suddenly there is a high-pitched sound.)

VICKI: What's that?

THE DOCTOR: A signal that the ship is charged, unless I'm much mistaken.

STEVEN: I hope so.

(The sound stops.)

CHUMBLEY: You are right, Doctor. We are ready to disconnect.

(THE DOCTOR, STEVEN and VICKI all sigh with relief. A CHUMBLEY comes in with the end of the cable.)

THE DOCTOR: Are you sure you have enough power?

CHUMBLEY: Enough to get us well out into space, where we can recharge from a sun.

THE DOCTOR: Good. Good. Well, that's all. We can go.

CHUMBLEY: A Chumbley will escort you back to your ship.

THE DOCTOR: And you?

CHUMBLEY: We will wait until you are safely there.

THE DOCTOR: We shall be all right. You need time to get out of range. We don't. The moment I start my ship we are out of range in time. We need no space.

VICKI: Go now. Please.

CHUMBLEY: Very well. In a moment we shall leave here and enter the ship. From that time we will not be able to talk with you. The Chumbley with you will escort you to your ship. He will protect you and obey your commands. Once you have gone he will destroy himself.

VICKI: Oh, no!

CHUMBLEY: It will be painless. Merely putting itself out of action.

THE DOCTOR: I understand. Thank you for your help.

CHUMBLEY: It is easy to help others when they are so willing to help you. Though we are beings of separate planets, you from the solar system and we from another space, our ways of thought, at times, do not seem all that different. It has been an honour to know you and serve you.

THE DOCTOR: Hmm.

VICKI: Good luck.

CHUMBLEY: Thank you. We shall give you time to get clear before we take off. Now we are going. Goodbye. We wish you well.

(There is a click, a humming noise starts and the chamber trembles.)

THE DOCTOR: They've started the motors.

STEVEN: Less than half an hour.

THE DOCTOR: Yes, quite right.

23. Exterior.

(MAAGA, DRAHVIN ONE and DRAHVIN TWO are sitting on the ground, dirty and dishevelled.)

DRAHVIN ONE: Where are the machines?

DRAHVIN TWO: There are none.

MAAGA: Listen.

(There is a humming sound which gradually increases to a roar.)

They are escaping.

(They leap to their feet. As they do the roar reaches a climax, and as they squint up into the sky, a brilliant light flickers over them.)

24. EXTERIOR.

(Nearby THE DOCTOR, STEVEN *and* VICKI *are looking up into the sky, also bathed in the flickering light, and deafened by the roaring of the spaceship's engines.)*

STEVEN: There they go.

THE DOCTOR: Amazing. Amazing.

*(*THE DOCTOR *appears lost in thought.* VICKI, *mindful of how little time is left, urges* THE DOCTOR *on.)*

VICKI: Doctor!

THE DOCTOR: Yes, yes, come along.

(They turn away, as the roaring gradually fades away.)

25. EXTERIOR.

*(*MAAGA *and the* DRAHVINS *see* THE DOCTOR, STEVEN *and* VICKI.*)*

MAAGA: Quickly! The Earth people. We can stop them!

*(*THE DOCTOR, STEVEN *and* VICKI *hasten across the landscape. A* CHUMBLEY *chitters about them. Suddenly the* CHUMBLEY *stops, turns around and fires as the* DRAHVINS *attack. There is a bright flash and the* DRAHVINS *fling themselves to the*

ground.)

26. *EXTERIOR THE TARDIS.*

(STEVEN and VICKI run towards the ship, clearly out of breath.)

STEVEN: Come on.

VICKI: The suns will be up in a moment.

(THE DOCTOR runs up, panting for breath, grasping the side of the police box to steady himself. The CHUMBLEY is just behind him.)

THE DOCTOR: Time is running out.

(THE DOCTOR pushes open the door and they go in, avoiding the cable that leads away from the ship. STEVEN comes out again with the end of the cable and tosses it to the ground. The door closes again. The DRAHVINS rush towards the ship, their guns blazing. It is getting lighter now as dawn fast approaches. The TARDIS gradually dematerialises. MAAGA and the DRAHVINS stagger back, clasping their hands over their ears, surprised by the sound it makes. The planet starts to shake, more violently than ever, and MAAGA and the DRAHVINS look around, fear etched on their faces. As the planet begins to break up, the

noise is deafening.)

27. INTERIOR THE *TARDIS*.

(THE DOCTOR is busy manipulating the controls of the ship. STEVEN and VICKI are looking very relieved at their escape.)

STEVEN: Can we see the disintegration on the scanner?

THE DOCTOR: No, I'm afraid we've already dematerialised from that galaxy.

(VICKI still looks up at the scanner. THE DOCTOR watches her and moves to join her.)

What is it, Vicki?

VICKI: I've hurt my ankle.

THE DOCTOR: Have you? Well, I'll look at it in a moment. It would be nice to find a place where we could stop and take stock of ourselves. To be free of dangers for just a little while.

(VICKI points up at the scanner, which shows whole galaxies of stars.)

VICKI: Perhaps that one, the bright star at the top...

(THE DOCTOR smiles and turns to

STEVEN.*)*

THE DOCTOR: Flick that red lever on.

(STEVEN *does so*. THE DOCTOR *turns back to* VICKI.)

VICKI: I wonder what is going on on that planet.

THE DOCTOR: Yes, I wonder...

(*A million stars fill the screen, then the scanner fills with a closer shot, as a planet, not the one they have just left, is isolated.*)

28. *EXTERIOR A JUNGLE (NIGHT).*

(GARVEY *lays on his back on the floor of the jungle, barely conscious. There is a terrifying animal screech and he opens his eyes with a start.*)

GARVEY: I remember now... remember... I must kill... kill... kill.

Next Episode:
MISSION TO THE UNKNOWN

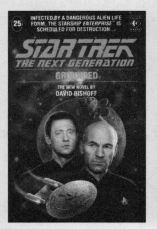

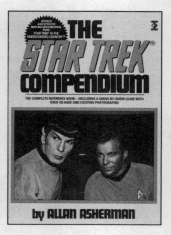

For a complete list of Titan's Doctor Who publications,
please send a large stamped SAE to Titan Books Mail
Order, 42-44 Dolben Street, London SE1 0UP.
Please quote reference DW9 on both envelopes.